T0383614

Creating Equity and Access

for Gifted Learners

Creating Equity and Access for Gifted Learners provides an overview of how and why to implement the ExCEL Problem-Based Learning Instruction Model as a change initiative in classrooms and the impact that this model has had on gifted programs.

As the product of evidence from two federally-funded Jacob K. Javits grants, the ExCEL Model is a systemic, design-based, continuous improvement curriculum and professional learning program that closes equity gaps for culturally, linguistically, and economically diverse students by increasing effective problem-based learning (PBL) instruction. This book provides readers with the background, evidence, and tools necessary to implement the program model as a change initiative in their schools. Learn how to implement effective, research-grounded professional learning, demonstrate best practice, and navigate red tape and roadblocks.

Full of immediately implementable strategies and lesson examples, this book is a must-have resource for district leaders, instructional leaders, and teachers who are ready to make their dream of implementing an equitable and effective professional learning program a reality.

Anne K. Horak, PhD taught middle school and served as a K-12 administrator supervising advanced programs prior to serving as a Principal Investigator and Project Director for Project ExCEL and ExCEL-Ignite. She has written multiple book chapters and articles and has contributed to the development of award-winning PBL curriculum units.

Kimberley Daly, PhD serves as Coordinator for Project ExCEL-Ignite, a federally-funded grant at George Mason University that seeks to identify culturally, linguistically, and economically diverse students for gifted programs through problem-based learning (PBL). Dr. Daly has 30 years of educational experience. Her research focuses on PBL, advanced academics, and global citizenship.

Shannon King, PhD has worked in education for 30 years as a classroom teacher, gifted education teacher, instructional coach, and administrator. She also works as an Adjunct Professor at George Mason University, teaching courses in curriculum and instruction, assessment and differentiation, gifted education, and educational research.

Creating Equity and Access

for Gifted Learners

Implementing a Problem-Based Professional
Learning Experience Using the ExCEL Model

Anne K. Horak, Kimberley Daly, and
Shannon King

Routledge
Taylor & Francis Group

NEW YORK AND LONDON

Designed cover image: Alexandra Veatch | Letterpress Communications

First published 2025
by Routledge
605 Third Avenue, New York, NY 10158

and by Routledge
4 Park Square, Milton Park, Abingdon, Oxon, OX14 4RN

Routledge is an imprint of the Taylor & Francis Group, an informa business

ISBN: 978-1-032-58988-6 (hbk)
ISBN: 978-1-032-58784-4 (pbk)
ISBN: 978-1-003-45246-1 (ebk)

DOI: 10.4324/9781003452461

Typeset in Adobe Caslon Pro
by Newgen Publishing UK

Dedication

To Bev
Who carried the light high ahead of us without casting her shadow over us.

Contents

Foreword

The history of gifted child education has been relatively short within the overall timeframe of research: about 120 years, with the first official report (e.g., Marland Report) to the US Congress not being published until 1972. Throughout that time, there have been debates on what is giftedness, who is gifted, how do we identify it, and how do we serve these students? Beginning with the civil rights era in the 1970s, these questions expanded to focus on how broad the range of gifted students really is and why everyone is not included. Our models for identification, historically situated in the testing movements, also exacerbated the ability to find and serve students from diverse populations. The upshot was to try new and different tests, expand student services, prepare teachers and parents as potential informants, and engage all students in curricular adaptations.

A critical relationship within all of the efforts to expand access has the collaboration between the designs for implementation (which often rely heavily on the classroom teacher, the students, and the content to be delivered. The depth and willingness of teachers to engage is crucial for the success of any implementation, that is, it must *make sense* and have fidelity with district standards. Teachers need to see the implementation as worthy of the time and effort it takes, beneficial to their students, and supported by administration.

Some of the early designs were implemented in segments and a few were implemented as comprehensive approaches. Project ExCEL is one of the most comprehensive approaches to the identification and service of diverse middle school students, with the goal of providing long-term access to engaging and rich opportunities for learning throughout high school.

The unique elements of Project ExCEL rest in the curriculum-aligned problem-based learning units, which are scaffolded by in-depth and continuous professional learning for teachers. This combination situates problem-based learning as a dynamic assessment method, resulting in universal screening for diverse middle school students. Teacher action and engagement through ongoing professional learning, collaboration, and metacognitive coaching result in a sustainable model for students and teachers alike. Project ExCEL didn't end with its first round of funding; using the research-based evidence derived from the ExCEL Model, it evolved to become Project ExCEL-Ignite to continue the work across regions and states. The advantage of time has allowed our research team to configure the very best of what we *know* in gifted child education to create a unique, innovative, and compelling program for middle school students. At the same time, it has created an environment for teachers to see students differently, find their strengths, and realize that all students can benefit from PBL as a challenging curriculum. They actually like their teaching more. Project ExCEL has literally changed their perspectives on teaching, students, and accessibility.

This is the story of how it all happened through the contributions, hard work, and commitment of classroom teachers, administrators, and the George Mason University team. This is the story of the thoughts of diverse middle school students and how they felt heard and seen during the PBL curriculum. This is also the story of the barriers encountered during the pandemic of 2020, the renewal of commitments, and the continuation of the project. This is a story of change.

The issues of access and equity in education continue. The need for all teachers to engage and support access continues. What we have learned is that change is supported by comprehensive and long-term models that support stakeholders. Change does not come because we say *change*; it comes the same way that learning does, whether the teacher is the learner or the student is the learner.

I have had the advantage of serving as a colleague, consultant, and mentor to this team. After some 30 years in education, much of it in teacher education and gifted child education, it has been a privilege to work with a new generation of researchers in the field. Researchers who are not limited by the boundaries of narrow definitions or traditions and researchers who use participatory action research to work with their teacher colleagues in the classroom to refine the model for success. The comprehensive nature of this program is astounding, embedded in middle school classrooms across regions and states with substantive curriculum, teachers who are heavily invested, and students who develop self-efficacy and, more importantly self-advocacy. What more could you ask? The long-term commitment of the team and the sustainability of the project leadership have also been factors in its success: stability supports fidelity.

I invite you to read more about Project ExCEL and its sister, Project ExCEL-Ignite.

Find out:

◈ The critical elements you need in your classroom and school to provide accessibility for students through challenging and interesting PBL curriculum;

◈ The critical elements that allow you to see your students for all of their potential and talent;

◈ The difference between one-shot professional development and long-term professional learning for teachers;

◈ How to engage students and enhance teaching through PBL while focusing on student achievement; and

◈ How to enjoy teaching and learning again.

All my best,
Beverly Shaklee

Preface

If you are reading this, you may be a teacher of gifted, honors, or advanced academics or a general education teacher interested in trying something new and different. You may be an instructional coach or GT (Gifted and Talented) resource teacher looking to support the professional growth of your team and school. You may be a district gifted coordinator or supervisor grappling with underrepresentation and looking for the change that will make your program equitable. Or you may be a scholar in the field of gifted education looking to ground your work in evidence. You are in the right place!

We have been there. Together, we had one guiding Polaris: to make lives better for teachers and students. That is why we are here. As classroom teachers, we wanted to make our professional lives and the lives of our students better by energizing ourselves with something new, like problem-based learning curriculum. In the role of GT resource teachers and instructional coaches, we strived to make the ecosystem of schools better by supporting teacher professional growth and dismantling the achievement versus engagement dichotomy. In positions supporting district programs, we endeavored to build infrastructure to initiate and sustain transformative change. In our capacity as scholars, our mission was to replicate the model with fidelity and disseminate it for the broadest impact.

This brings us back to you. If you are a teacher of gifted, honors, or advanced academic students or general education students, this book will provide you with an understanding of problem-based learning, how it is different from project-based learning or what you are already doing, and how the specific things that make it different have a profoundly positive impact in the classroom. If you are an instructional coach or GT resource teacher, this book will provide you with the tools and information you need to support your teachers in their professional growth and guide your school in increasing student achievement using curriculum characterized by engaging high-level instruction. If you are a district gifted coordinator or supervisor, this book will provide you with a road map for how to implement and sustain an evidence-based continuous improvement program model: a model that delivers transformational results in increasing equity and access within identification for gifted programs while providing comprehensive support for professional learning and curriculum development. If you are a scholar, you will find evidence broadening the literature base that supports research on increasing equity and access within identification and effective professional learning for educators.

We invite you to meet us where you are. You may read this book as a professional self-help book and feel inspired by the wisdom we share to seek out more resources to implement problem-based learning. You may read this book as a manual to learn the steps and skills required to implement a curriculum-aligned and problem-based professional learning program, designed to support teacher reflection and professional growth, and persuade your school to come on board with this program. You may read this book as a research brief in order to develop a rationale for investing time and resources in bringing this program to scale. You may read this book as a journal article in order to understand the research and evidence that supports the model.

This may seem ambitious. Tackling the severity of issues like underrepresentation, supporting teacher professional growth, and the development of high-level curriculum all at once can be overwhelming. The truth is that this book cannot do it all. A book is not a critical peer who can provide feedback that prompts reflection. A book is not a collaborative group that discusses what they hope to accomplish and creates goals to support the realization of that vision. A book is not an expert consultant who can provide evaluative feedback and evidence-based programmatic support. A book is not a team of researchers who can analyze data and evaluate implications. These components emerge from our sustained work with schools. This book was designed to be a launching pad for that work. You could do this work alone with what you take away from this book, but what we know to be true is that the experience is amplified by the guiding hand of a team of experts working by your side. Work we continue to this day. Work we invite you to do with us.

Acknowledgements

It would be remiss of us if we did not first thank all of the brave teachers and schools. They took the risk and came on board with Project ExCEL and, later, Project ExCEL-Ignite. We learned from them. The model is better because of them.

We would like to thank our editors Rebecca, Alex, and Quinn for noticing this work and guiding us toward making it a valuable resource for educators.

We would like to thank the Program Officers of the US Department of Education Office of Well-Rounded Education, Office of Elementary and Secondary Education Jacob K. Javits Education for their support and encouragement. Gay Ojugbana and Jeannette Horner-Smith have been champions of this work all along, giving us support and guidance as we carried out our program objectives. Without this critical funding in place to begin with, the ExCEL Model would never have emerged from the broader implementation it took to collect, analyze, and evaluate data that provided insights into the critical outcomes.

That being said, this book contains examples and resource materials that are provided for the reader's convenience. The opinions expressed in any of these materials do not necessarily reflect the positions or policies of the US Department of Education. *George Mason University's Project ExCEL (2014) (S206A140022) and Project ExCEL-Ignite (2019) (S206A190025) are US Department of Education's Jacob K. Javits Gifted and Talented Students Education Program funded projects. All content included or made available through this book, such as text, graphics, logos, and images, is the exclusive intellectual property of Project ExCEL and Project ExCEL-Ignite and is protected by federal policy regulating the administration of the projects.*

We would like to thank the George Mason University College of Education and Human Development. Mason brought us together and gave us a platform from which we were able to launch our movement.

Thanks also go to Alex and Ilsa at Letterpress Communications for seeing the growth potential in our project and taking us on despite its size. Thank you for seeing the way forward and pushing us to the next level.

We would like to thank our research assistants. A book like this does not come to fruition without a dedicated team of students who assist with all aspects of Project ExCEL and Project ExCEL-Ignite, including organizing curriculum, measures, and data for teachers and schools, helping the project team to prepare for professional learning sessions, and conducting literature reviews and checking materials. We are indebted to these doctoral and undergraduate students who have invested time, effort, and heart into creating equity for students. We take pride in the small part that we have had in their program and are excited for their future success.

We would like to thank our gifted and other academic colleagues. Colleagues near and far informed our work and are often walking parallel paths in other states to make the lives of teachers and students better.

It is hard to imagine where we would be without Becca. During the early years, she held everything together with a little bit of duct tape and love. Her commitment and professional knowledge nurtured the development of this project into something stable.

There are no words adequate enough to express our admiration and affection for Bev Shaklee. Bev took us all under her wing and under her wing was a very good place to be. Imagine a colleague who is also your boss, your mother, your best friend, and a superhero. Then, you have the faintest idea of what it is like to be one of Bev's chosen ones. The very fact that this book exists is a testament to her mentorship and excellence. Bev knew when to lead the way, when to step out of the way, and when to push us on our way. Bev, your legacy is that we will strive to "pull a Bev" in all things we do.

No one has lost more blood, sweat, and tears over this project than our award-winning curriculum writer Dana Plowden. Her gains and losses were both professional and personal. Yet, through it all, this project was her passion. We all know that writing is your career and teaching pays the bills. Remember Williamsburg? Someday, it will be more than a fairy tale celebration. We love you, Dana.

We would like to thank our mothers, those still with us and those who are not. Particularly Linda Maselli, who, at times, kept two young grandchildren occupied virtually for hours on end during school closures and let everyone on the team know that they were included in her family.

Nearest and dearest to our heart, we would like to thank our families. A book like this does not get written in the span of time it takes to put the words down on paper. It takes all the missed date nights, doctor's appointments, birthday parties, and special events that were the unintended consequences of dedicating a career to creating equity. Our families know better than anyone that while sometimes we had to prioritize them and sometimes we had to prioritize work, we always strived to know which one to do when. Jere, Mike, David, Emily, and Matthew, even when we did not get it exactly right, you were always more important to us than anything else.

Introduction

Anne Horak

How the ExCEL Model Came To Be: Anne

Dana Plowden and I hunched over the large three-ring binder. We were in our early years as teachers. Our assistant principal had suggested we work together on lesson planning. There were state standards and district standards. How did it all go together? What was the same? What was different? Importantly, what was on the test? Even more so, what wasn't? We were supposed to extend lessons for advanced students. But, how? Using what standards?

After school, on a sunny afternoon just after the start of school in September, we met in Dana's eighth-grade English language arts classroom on the second floor of the middle school. Rays of afternoon sunlight striated the floor and warmed the student desks where we sat puzzling. We were trying to figure out how we could engage students with meaningful instruction while keeping in mind standards, achievement, accountability, and individual needs for scaffolding or extension. Everything I have done since, for students and for teachers, stemmed from the powerful motivation of that early curiosity.

 DOI: 10.4324/9781003452461-1

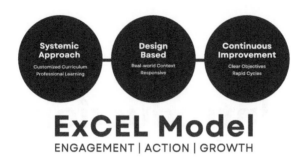

Figure 0.1 The ExCEL Model.

Project ExCEL-Ignite | Letterpress Communications

For more than a decade, Shannon King, Kimberley Daly, and I have worked in pursuit of similar purposes. Early in our careers, we were classroom teachers in different states and countries, yet the concerns about education that preoccupied our work overlapped. Eventually, our trajectories intersected in Virginia, where we all worked for the same school system and pursued a doctoral degree at the same university. I met Shannon working in the central office where we served as advocates for gifted children and teacher professional learning. I met Kim in graduate class. She and I taught English language arts in schools characterized by culturally, linguistically, and economically diverse students. Though I did not know her then, I taught seventh grade in the feeder middle school to her high school. Kim taught in the International Baccalaureate Diploma Programme. Like me, she was interested in concept-based and inquiry instruction, as well as rigorous high-level curriculum. Shannon, Kim, and Dana are a part of the community that makes the work implementing the ExCEL Model exist and evolve. Their expertise gives momentum to the growth of the model. Their perspectives add depth and clarity. This community is invaluable to the success of the model and includes others who will come into play as this story unfolds. And yet, I began my career as an individual teacher working in isolation with a restless desire to do better by my students.

And so, I will start with that.

I began my teaching career in Charlotte, North Carolina, in 1997. At the time, the state of North Carolina was deep in an attempt to grapple with the accountability standards that had been foisted upon our US education system. Though it feels familiar now, at the time, North Carolina was ahead of other states with their testing trajectory. The State Education Department had mandated end of grade testing; then, districts had ramped up to semester testing and, later, quarterly testing. End of year bonuses were tied to scores on these tests.

The demographics of my school were clustered at either end of the socioeconomic spectrum. There was a population of wealthy White families that lived in the coveted Myers' Park area and poor, mostly Black families that lived in the subsided housing developments on South Boulevard near Interstate 77. It was the diverse lower socio-economic population that concerned our school leadership. With changes in boundaries and bussing, this demographic was new to the school. The entitlement of the existing population emerged in emotionally charged conflicts. There was pressure on our principal to ensure that our test scores demonstrated that the rigor and reputation of the school had not changed.

Amid this complicated social and political dynamic, I was a youthful, energetic, novice teacher, filled with optimism and idealism. I believed if you engaged students, they would learn. I believed all students could learn. I believed if you had high expectations, the students would rise to them. I believed if you taught higher level thinking skills, the facts and standards would fall into place. At that time, I was also 22 years old and supporting myself in a state more than 400 miles from my family and safety net. Regardless of what I dreamed could be, I conformed to what was expected.

This included daily warm-ups of previously released End-of-Grade (EOG) test questions in my sixth-grade English language arts class. I combed through released tests to find questions that aligned to the objectives I was teaching. I thought I had hit the jackpot when I found one question that had been on the test three years in a row. Though the reading passage had changed, the question remained the same. Even now, more than 20 years later, I still remember the question almost verbatim. It was, "What does the author do to support reader understanding?" The answer was, "uses text structures, such as headings and subheadings." Elated, I made a transparency of the question. Just the question. I put the transparency on the overhead. For my warm-up that morning, I had my students copy the question and the answer. I said, "There is a question that has been on the EOG three years in a row. The answer is the same regardless of the reading passage. This is the question. This is the answer. Memorize it."

Even as I wrote the directions for the warm-up on the board, even as the students filed in and took their seats, pulled out their notebooks, sharpened their pencils, and even as I stepped into place in the front of the classroom and flipped on the overhead, I thought to myself, "This isn't teaching." Transparency and projector aside, I have no doubt that this story resonates on some level with many, even now when our response to accountability has evolved to become more sophisticated. The problem for me was not so much the testing itself, but that the window was closing on the variety of methods we could use to teach students in the service of success on those tests.

And yet, I needed a job. This is what I had spent four years in higher education learning to do. I found what I believed to be an escape route. A colleague of mine had moved to Northern Virginia the previous year. I visited her during a week between when school was closed for me but still in session for her. I interviewed with the assistant principal and was hired. Virginia was not yet at the point where the state had ramped up testing to the same frequency as North Carolina. I thought it was my chance to teach the way I wanted to teach before things got bad. I hoped Virginia would take a different route.

I was hired at a school with a Gifted and Talented center program since I had completed master's level gifted endorsement classes at the University of North Carolina at Charlotte. The district had a newly conceived plan to expand its advanced academics program. I expressed my interest in this area by participating in summer curriculum development projects. Following this, I was recruited to apply to a district-level position to develop, expand, implement, and support this program at the middle school level. It was a time of significant and meaningful change for the district. This meant moving from a special magnet center program to a program at every middle school and moving from a highly selective screening process to the addition of an open enrollment option for middle school courses. It was an exciting time to be part of a dynamic team in a place that had resources and access to the best thinkers and scholars in the field of gifted education.

My passion and purpose for this came from my experience. My older sister had required significant special educational intervention. In comparison, it was a relief to my parents that my grades and progress were consistent and sufficient. Because my sister's needs were more urgent, the limited time and attention they had mostly went to supporting her. Special educational services in this era were not as robustly available. In this context, I felt overlooked. While I was successful at meeting expectations, there were no challenges, extensions, or enrichment in my educational career. No one pushed me and I did not push myself. In this context, I felt underestimated.

This experience is likely why I felt an affinity for serving gifted students. It was important to me to leverage the opportunity for broader impact. The belief driving my vision was that all students deserved opportunities and those that rose to the challenge were entitled to have their potential cultivated. Basically, no one should be overlooked or underestimated.

An Overview of Underrepresentation

As is well documented, being overlooked and underestimated in the field of gifted education has meant that culturally, linguistically, and economically diverse students have been systematically excluded from gifted programs. Girls and students with disabilities have been left out too, but not to the same extent. Gifted programs have had a long history of underrepresentation. To understand this phenomenon, we need to understand a little bit about how gifted identification has traditionally been done and why we need something different.

Historically, giftedness was considered innate, that is, something a person was born with. This is what we think of as a fixed or unitary notion of giftedness. Because educators thought giftedness was a static trait, they focused on finding tests that would clearly indicate whether a child was gifted or not. As a result, school districts began using tests, such as IQ tests, to identify giftedness. Historically, IQ tests were created and normed for White children from middle- to upper-income families. There was an innate bias in the testing that we still have not overcome. School district personnel often administered these tests only once or twice throughout a student's entire 12-year career in public school. This meant that if their test scores did not identify them as gifted in second or third grade, many students were never retested and, therefore, never considered gifted or given access to services.

Complicating this system is the trend toward student mobility. If students enroll in a new school after second or third grade, they will most likely never be identified or tested. In the US, the most highly mobile students are Black, Latinx, and children of poverty. This means, given the systemic constraints, that these populations are less likely to be tested and less likely to be identified. This leads to a disproportionate number of culturally, linguistically, and economically diverse children in gifted programs. As educators, we have seen this identification system exclude many students who were potentially gifted. As a result, many identification policies have changed to include an option for parents or teachers to refer a student for testing. While this has been a step forward, it still does not go far enough. Research data indicate (McBee, 2006; Siegle, 2016) that referrals do not consistently happen in secondary school. In fact, after elementary school, few students are identified. In addition, parents who are vulnerable because they may not understand enough or feel comfortable navigating the school system rarely request referrals. Therefore, adding parent referrals only benefits a small handful of students whose parents have the resources to be strong advocates.

The Strategies and Activities

I was working in central office. I was part of a team relentlessly working to impact this deeply entrenched issue. As we saw it, we had three imperatives to address. We needed to influence identification policy, explore practice, and examine procedures. Of his architectural style, Frank Lloyd Wright said, "Form and function should be one, joined in a spiritual union." When applied to our work, this meant that we could not separate these imperatives. Our team needed to be working on all fronts at once, advocating with leadership for policy change, negotiating beliefs about instruction with curriculum specialists, and broadening perspectives on students for teachers. Change of this magnitude, particularly in education, requires support on many levels. And support on many levels requires evidence.

Policies

We collaborated with Dr. Beverly Shaklee to use her evidence-based model, the Early Assessment of Exceptional Potential (EAEP), to develop more inclusive identification policies that reflected a whole-child approach. Dr. Shaklee had previously worked with a team of researchers at Kent State University to develop a dynamic performance assessment model to look at the whole child for gifted potential. The EAEP is based on the premise that children may reveal the attributes identified in the literature as evidence of giftedness in different ways, based on their exposure, culture, and environment. The EAEP uses a framework of four categories, including Exceptional Learner (or the acquisition of information), Exceptional User (or the application of information), Exceptional Generator (or the adaption of information), and Exceptional Motivation (or the intensity in the desire to know). Teachers make observations over time grounded in this model. These observations are then triangulated with other data, such as products students make while engaged in high-level rigorous curriculum experiences.

Practice

This necessitated the development of high-level rigorous curriculum that would elicit student performances aligned to the EAEP framework. Our team collaborated with Dr. Shelagh Gallagher on a problem-based learning (PBL) curriculum initiative. Dr. Gallagher provided summer institutes for PBL curriculum development. As a part of this initiative, Dana Plowden worked with Dr. Gallagher as an apprentice writer for many years. As a result, the district developed the most robust PBL curriculum initiative available.

Procedures

To pull together these changes in policy and practice, professional learning was provided for teachers, administrators, and instructional leaders. The focus of this professional learning was to communicate and establish the new policies for identification and support teacher growth with changes to the curriculum and their instruction.

All of the pieces for meaningful change on many levels were in place. At the system level, we had policies that had changed. At the school level, we had concrete curriculum in place for teachers to implement. In between, we had advocates and infrastructure to support it all. People argue whether top down or grassroots initiatives are the best way for change to take place. Well, our work suggests that it is more than that. Change happens with support on many levels: top down, bottom up, inside out, and outside in.

The Theory of Change Guiding Implementation

In its shortest form, the theory of change is based on something Jim Gallagher was known to say often. That was, you do not need a test to find a gifted student. You know it when you see it.

Therefore, the theory of change is if teachers learn how to implement PBL curriculum, these teachers will implement PBL. During implementation, teachers will observe emergent critical and creative problem-solving skills. Teachers will triangulate these observations and align these data to the EAEP model to make systemic, grounded, and evidence-based recommendations of students that will result in enrollment in advanced courses reflecting the more equitable representation of historically excluded students.

This is an inductive reasoning approach. Behavior that reflects advanced capacity is complex. Teachers synthesize specific examples to make broader generalizations. It is additive. Teachers consider whether the number of instances and observations that reach a critical mass establish patterns. It is holistic. Teachers use professional judgement to evaluate the meaning that emerges from looking at the whole picture in context.

Evidence leans away from using teachers' professional judgement. Researchers bear responsibility for this. In order to capture teacher input while bearing in mind time constraints, researchers developed checklists. Yet, checklists are remissive. They limit examples of advanced performance to a specific set of indicators. They require teachers to test observations against a static list of indicators. This is a deductive reasoning approach. It is analytical. Complex behavior is divided into parts or elements. The context for evaluating meaning is lost. Therefore, a consistent result is not predictable. From a research perspective, when a result is random, it is not reliable.

Researchers had good intentions. Checklists reflected sound research. The problem was not the checklist in and of itself, but the professional judgement that was lost in the process of evaluating the meaning of behaviors in context. Now we know better. And we should do better.

Desired Impact

The ExCEL Model is a system of ideas that has been proven to effective by a continuous line of federally-funded research supported by the US DOE Jacob K Javits program. We have had two projects, beginning with Project ExCEL (Shaklee & Horak, 2014) and continuing with Project ExCEL-Ignite (Horak & Shaklee, 2019). This book is an account of what we have learned as a result of these two projects. In the pages that follow, the model's positive achievement and engagement outcomes will speak for themselves. There is also something to learn from our experience of bringing change to schools.

Someone once asked me if I wanted problem-based learning to take over. I found it an odd question. As if I were staging a coup. I was curious whether the questioner found current practice so meaningful, fulfilling, and effective that it would be irreplaceable. Certainly, for me, it was not. Problem-based learning is a vehicle to create learning environments where no child is overlooked, no child is underestimated, and no teacher is burned out. All these years later, I am not sure whether that thought was profoundly ambitious or profoundly unexceptional. If that requires a problem-based curriculum and professional learning coup, then here it is.

References

Horak, A., & Shaklee, B. (2019). *Project E-Ignite*. U.S. Department of Education, Javits Gifted and Talented Students Education Grant Program.

McBee, M. T. (2006). A descriptive analysis of referral sources for gifted identification screening by race and socioeconomic status. *Journal of Secondary Gifted Education, 17,* 103–111. https://doi.org/10.4219/jsge-2006-686

Shaklee, B., & Horak, A. (2014). *Project ExCEL.* U.S. Department of Education, Institute of Educational Sciences, Javits Gifted and Talented Students Education Grant Program.

Siegle, D. (2016, January 11-12). *Research Update from the NCRGE,* [Presentation]. Jacob K. Javits Gifted and Talented Student Education Program Project Directors' Meeting, Washington, D.C. United States. https://ncrge.uconn.edu/wp-content/uploads/sites/982/2016/01/Center-Slides-for-Javits-Jan-2016-Meeting.pdf

An Introduction to Problem-Based Learning

Chapter 1

Problem-Based Learning: An Ace on First Serve

Kimberley Daly

Shared Values

I first met Anne Horak when we were both students in our doctoral program. We were taking the same program evaluation course and for 15 weeks, we were part of a group of students refining our research skills. I remember Anne was keenly focused on problem-based learning (PBL). I also knew that we worked for the same Virginia school district and she was also a former English teacher. Until that point, we had not crossed paths.

I began my education career in 1995. My first teaching job was at a high school just a few blocks away from the Holland Tunnel in New Jersey. My students did not have access to a library, computers, or a gym on site. Many did not have stable home lives and some worried about gang violence. Almost all of them lived in poverty. This first

 DOI: 10.4324/9781003452461-3

experience impressed upon me the need to provide *every* student with a chance and an opportunity. As a teacher, I pushed my students to look toward the future and be successful despite the hardships they had. This core belief is one I have kept with me and continues to guide my work.

After several years teaching in New Jersey, I moved to Virginia. I worked for a large suburban school district and taught secondary English and International Baccalaureate (IB) Diploma Programme coursework. Once again, I found myself being drawn to equity and opportunity.

The high school in Virginia where I worked encouraged students to take IB courses rather than using traditional gatekeeping to control access to them. I loved the idea of students being provided with opportunities rather than barriers and I pushed students to take my IB English class whenever possible. The International Baccalaureate curriculum is rigorous and high level. It drives students to think critically and creatively. Students who complete IB coursework are ultimately well-prepared for whatever they choose to do next, whether it be college, the military, or entering the workforce.

Years later, Anne and I crossed paths again when we ended up working at the same institution where we earned our degrees. Anne designed and conducted educational research and I taught education courses for pre- and in-service teachers. Dr. Beverly Shaklee, someone we both respected greatly and worked with separately, reintroduced Anne and me. As we got to know each other, we found that our work and values were complementary. The same belief that I had found that Anne and I shared when we met in our doctoral program was still there when Anne and I started working together. This became particularly apparent when we were writing a proposal for the Javits and the premise of our proposal centered on the question at the heart of our core belief: how can we expand access and opportunity while keeping in mind issues that impact equity?

Tackling Educational Change

There has always been pressure for schools to change. Policymakers, state and national leadership, parents, and other stakeholders have always pushed districts and schools to adapt, innovate, and adopt various initiatives, some mandated by legislation, some by changing technologies or a desire to be competitive with other countries, and others by a sincere desire to improve the skills and knowledge of students. Despite the many initiatives adopted and implemented in school districts around the US – where gains have been achieved – sadly, many have not been able to scale up.

Anne and I knew this all too well. Everyone involved in our two federal grant projects had spent significant time in the classroom teaching students. We all sat through countless professional learning sessions to introduce the latest curriculum trend or initiative to raise student achievement scores. What we learned from our experiences is that meaningful educational change requires three things: districts and schools to create the conditions for educational change to happen, teachers to be open to changing their practice, add implementation to be supported by professional learning and sustained opportunities for feedback and support.

Tennis, Teachers, and PBL

I am a former tennis player and an avid fan. Major tournaments are two weeks of excitement throughout which players will rise and fall. For a player on a tennis court, games, sets, and matches are the culmination of forehands, backhands, slices, serves, and lobs. Each rally is made up of different strokes and the best players can choose the exact spot where a tennis ball lands. The higher ranked players have a high percentage of successful points while lower ranked players, well, have fewer successful points.

When thinking about educational change, continuous and repeated successful serves, rallies, and points can lead to a set point and then, ultimately, the match. Problem-based learning can be an ace on first serve.

In tennis, an ace is a serve that lands in but is not hit at all by the receiving player. As a player, hitting an ace often causes a rush of adrenaline because of the suddenness of the point. Depending on when the ace was hit, a game could be turned or won, a set could be won, or a player could edge closer to match point. Aces are highly desired and aces on first serve are often exciting as players can hit balls with more force and aim for the corners of the service box. Aces thrill spectators and pump up the players.

Problem-based learning can be considered the pedagogy that is an ace on first serve. When teachers first learn about PBL in their professional learning, they become excited. When they start teaching it and students become curious, engaged, and inquisitive, teachers feel that surge of adrenaline. They notice new things about students. They see their classroom changing. As time goes on and they teach PBL more, they start to hit aces.

Making Educational Change Happen

These ideas are not too far out of line with educational change research. Michael Fullan, former dean of the University of Toronto and professor emeritus at the Ontario Institute for Studies in Education (OISE), has written extensively on educational change for more than 40 years. In his book *The NEW Meaning of Educational Change* (2016), he advocates for three phases in the change process: initiation, implementation, and continuation. I'll explain how he defines each phase and how it connects to what we believe in our work.

Initiation, Implementation, and Continuation

In Fullan's model of educational change, the first phase is **initiation**. This phase is sometimes called adoption or mobilization but generally, it consists of a process that leads up to and includes the decision to adopt some kind of change. This change can be initiated by one person or a group and it is usually connected to a desired outcome. For instance, a middle school principal may wish to improve reading scores on state assessments and decides to adopt a whole-school specific reading curriculum. Now, of course, some initiatives never end up getting started and decisions to adopt initiatives are influenced by other things, like policy, community support or pressure, funding, external actors, access, or teacher advocacy. Many potentially great programs do get adopted and even once adopted, they need to be implemented.

The next phase in Fullan's model is **implementation**. Implementation is the idea of putting into practice an idea, program, or set of structures new to the population and expected to help bring about or enact change. Often, this means a change to classroom practice in schools. Changes most likely occur with curriculum materials, beliefs about the curriculum and/or learning practice, or pedagogical methods. It is also possible for implementation to require changes to more than one of these factors. For schools, implementation is critical because it is the means of accomplishing the desired objective. In the case of the middle school principal I mentioned earlier, adopting a new whole-school reading curriculum to raise test scores may also require teachers to change their teaching practice and modify some of their beliefs about how students learn.

Implementation is often tricky. First, there are many factors that can influence the implementation of a new initiative. For the school or district that is adopting a new program, understanding the reasons for adoption is paramount. A few good questions to ask include:

◈   Why is this program/curriculum/pedagogy needed?

◈   Does everyone (teachers, administration, etc.) agree on and understand that need?

◈   What exactly is required to implement this new initiative?

◈   What other local or state priorities may complicate this implementation?

Once you have these answers, you can deal with any miscommunications or misunderstandings head-on and seek ways to provide for successful implementation.

Second, while teachers and others learn a new curriculum or pedagogy or change classroom practice, there are inescapable hiccups that will happen along the way. These hiccups often manifest as changes in confidence or classroom practice and occur when teachers experience a new program that requires new skills and understandings or changes in behavior. Over an initial period of time and with proper support, many of these issues can be smoothed out. This is important to ensure fidelity of implementation; in other words, all teachers, support staff, and others use the new initiative with their students in the same way.

Fullan's model concludes with **continuation**. This is also sometimes called institutionalization, but the focus here is really on sustainability. Once implementation is underway, a decision needs to be made about whether or not the project or initiative is being implemented effectively. For a school or district, this means that leadership must evaluate whether the project's objectives and goals are being met, whether there is general satisfaction with the project, and whether the project has moved grade levels, the school, or the district forward. Many projects that are not implemented effectively are later discontinued. Even with effective implementation, some projects may not be continued because of transitions or dwindling funding. A lack of interest at a higher level can also be a reason for discontinuation.

For projects that are sustained and continued, there are often specific factors that contribute to this. These include active leadership, professional learning, and efforts to include the project in larger initiatives (e.g., incorporating it into a broader area of district operations or including it in a strategic plan). For the principal I mentioned earlier, sustainability may mean visible support and troubleshooting for teachers during implementation, ongoing professional learning for teachers, or advocating for the program's inclusion in other initiatives at the district level.

Common Ground

As Anne and I started working together, we became familiar with each other's work. I learned about underrepresentation in gifted education and shared with her some of my experiences in advanced academics. We found common ground in how programs are implemented in schools. Anne drew on her experience in middle school and central office while I drew on my experiences in different types of schools offering various types of advanced programs. We had both been in education long enough to understand how Fullan's model could play out in the real-world conditions of schools.

As I learned more about problem-based learning from Anne, I also realized how well it fit in with other inquiry-based pedagogies I was familiar with. Problem-based learning, or PBL as it is commonly called, requires teachers to engage in cognitive apprenticeship with their students. Teachers are no longer *the sage on the stage* or bankers depositing knowledge (Freire, 2014). Problem-based learning develops content skills, critical thinking, and problem-solving skills. It aligns with state content standards. And PBL is engaging for students.

In short, problem-based learning affects educational change.

What Comes Next?

To really understand how problem-based learning affects educational change, it helps to take a deep dive into its technical specifications. To begin, I will walk through the components of the curriculum.

This will make clear what problem-based learning is and what it is not. I will explain how and why problem-based learning in particular is well suited to elicit higher level thinking in comparison to other instructional methods and strategies, which do not fare as well in this area. I'll also address some of the common concerns about implementing problem-based learning, such as standards alignment, and discuss specific benefits, such as its propensity to support transdisciplinarity, global citizenship, student self-direction, and future-ready skills that students need for success. I will also share experiences from PBL implementation. These positive research outcomes show increases in achievement and engagement. Most excitingly, and perhaps the reason you are reading this book, I will share how problem-based learning can be used as a curriculum intervention for educational change by implementing it as a universal screening method with a dynamic performance assessment to create access and equity in advanced classes.

References

Freire, P. (2014). *Pedagogy of the oppressed: 30ᵗʰ anniversary edition* (M. Bergman Ramos, Trans.) Bloomsbury.

Fullan, M. (2016). *The new meaning of educational change* (5th ed.). Teacher's College Press.

Chapter 2

What is Problem-Based Learning?

Kimberley Daly

Problem-Based Learning (PBL)

Problem-based learning (PBL) is an inquiry-based model of curriculum and instruction that uses an ill-structured problem to engage students' natural curiosity. It guides students to ask questions to ultimately learn about a specific topic in a core curriculum subject. Teachers engage in cognitive apprenticeship with students and work and learn together with their students. Teachers act as guides but students drive learning by asking questions, working together, conducting research, and reflecting on the learning process (Collins & Kapur, 2015).

Problem-based learning (PBL), as it is currently used in P-12 education, was originally adapted from medical schools. Over 40 years ago, Harold Barrows, a doctor and professor at McMaster University, noticed his students knew their content but struggled when interacting with patients. To help his students, Barrows converted his entire curriculum for the medical school into PBL. Working with real-world patient problems helped medical students to develop questioning skills, the ability to collaborate, and problem-solving skills.

 DOI: 10.4324/9781003452461-4

Later, the model developed by Barrows was adapted for P-12 education by Stepien and Pyke (1997) and follows five phases:

◈   Problem Engagement;
◈   Inquiry and Investigation;
◈   Problem Definition;
◈   Problem Resolution; and
◈   Problem Debrief.

Problem-based learning requires a shift in practice away from traditional, teacher-led instruction. It has three defining features: an ill-structured problem, the use of cognitive apprenticeship, and the student as a stakeholder. Each feature is important for PBL units to develop content, problem-solving, and critical thinking skills in students.

The ill-structured problem is what initiates instruction in a PBL unit. The problem is not unstructured, but instead carefully crafted to provide information at different points along the problem narrative (Horak, 2013). This allows students and teachers to decide the path of a class activity together, based on the information they have at the time. It also allows for more than one resolution.

Cognitive apprenticeship is also key to PBL. Teachers and students work and learn together. During the unit, the teacher models curiosity, creates opportunities for student self-directed learning, and prompts student reflection.

Finally, PBL has a student stakeholder. During a PBL unit, students have authority, responsibility, and accountability for the decisions being made concerning the problem narrative. Each decision should be made as a result of the information they receive, process, and synthesize.

The phases of problem-based learning and some example unit applications are provided below.

PROBLEM-BASED LEARNING

INSTRUCTIONAL ELEMENTS OF PROBLEM-BASED LEARNING

Problem-Based Learning (PBL) requires a shift in practice from traditional instruction. This highlights the three key instructional differences of PBL.

ILL-STRUCTURED PROBLEM
- Initiates the instruction
- Needs more information
- More than one resolution

COGNITIVE APPRENTICESHIP
- Models curiousity
- Creates self-directed learning
- Prompts reflection

STUDENT AS STAKEHOLDER
- Authority
- Responsibility
- Accountibility

PHASES OF PROBLEM-BASED LEARNING

PBL curriculum unfolds in sequences through the narrative of the problem.

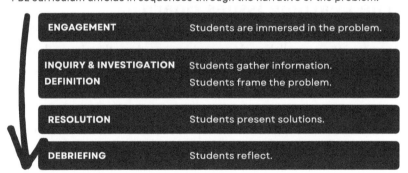

ENGAGEMENT	Students are immersed in the problem.
INQUIRY & INVESTIGATION	Students gather information.
DEFINITION	Students frame the problem.
RESOLUTION	Students present solutions.
DEBRIEFING	Students reflect.

Figure 2.1 The five phases of problem-based learning.

Project ExCEL-Ignite | Letterpress Communications

Problem Engagement

During the Problem Engagement phase of PBL, students are introduced to and immersed in the problem. The problem is ill-structured and has gaps in information. Often, problems are modeled on current issues or historical events. Either way, the problem is carefully crafted so that students also meet learning outcomes and content standards for their grade level. During Problem Engagement, the teacher and students also learn their stakeholder role. In a PBL unit, the stakeholder role can vary and the students and teacher can assume a different role for each unit. For example, in one unit, the class may be a web design team competing for a contract, while in another unit, they may be media consultants working on a presidential campaign.

At the beginning of every class session, the students and teacher revisit the problem and any additional information they have been given. To track the information and their work, a Learning Issues Board (LIB) is used.

The Learning Issues Board

The Learning Issues Board is an integral part of problem-based learning. It is a collaborative graphic organizer that is used at the beginning and end of every class session to organize information. In the PBL curriculum that we develop and use, the LIB is divided into three columns: 1) What We Know; 2) Learning Issues; and 3) Action Plan. There is also a space at the top of the board for the students and teacher to note any hunches that arise over the course of the unit. A sample template for the Learning Issues Board is provided below.

As information unfolds during the problem narrative, it should be listed in the What We Know column. As the teacher and students are in the same stakeholder role, it is important that the teacher facilitates what goes on the LIB through metacognitive coaching. The teacher's role is to drive students to identify the gaps in their knowledge. This means that the teacher should be careful not to tell students what

LEARNING ISSUES BOARD

Note hunches throughout the process.

WHAT WE KNOW	LEARNING ISSUES	ACTION PLAN

Figure 2.2 A sample Learning Issues Board.

Project ExCEL-Ignite | Letterpress Communications

is going on in the unit, but instead guide the students to drive their own learning by unpacking their own thoughts. One way in which the teacher accomplishes this is by answering student questions with questions.

The Learning Issues column is used for noting questions that come up over the course of the PBL unit. During the Problem Engagement phase, the teacher and students may receive several initial materials, including emails, formal documents, brochures, or other information. As the students and teacher process this information and put what they know on the LIB, questions also arise. These then form the starting points for the research that will be conducted during the next phase (Inquiry and Investigation).

The last column on the LIB is called Action Plan. This is where the teacher and students can put down their plan for answering the Learning Issues questions. For instance, if the students and teacher are members of a web development team, the final product may be a mockup of the website. The students and teacher need to collaboratively decide how to get from understanding the request from the client to creating the mockup. Ultimately, the Learning Issues Board is used to capture student ideas, help students to focus, and push students to explain their thinking throughout the PBL unit.

Inquiry and Investigation

This phase of a PBL unit allows students to reach a better understanding of the problem while they are in their stakeholder role. In most problem-based learning units, students conduct background research to help them to answer the questions they noted in the Learning Issues column of the LIB. As students obtain additional information during the problem narrative, it is possible that they will need to do more focused research to help them to understand how the additional information either constrains their work or provides additional things to consider. Students ultimately have to synthesize their knowledge and reflect on the validity of any information they receive.

Students build research, collaboration, and communication skills during the Inquiry and Investigation phase. As they find answers to their questions and sift through details, they may come across contradicting information. This will require students to share their findings, listen to and consider different perspectives, and prioritize information. For example, during a PBL unit in which students are in the stakeholder role of media consultants for a presidential candidate, they may watch television commercials and research previously televised presidential debates. Students may have different opinions about the candidate's strategies and messages in the media. These different messages and perspectives need to be cooperatively sorted through and students need to come to a consensus about the candidate's strategies.

Sometimes, units also spark connections to students' everyday lives that inspire research tangents that initially may not seem productive but, in the end, really contribute to the task required in the unit. One of my favorite stories from a teacher came from when she was implementing a PBL unit focused on healthy and non-healthy food options. In the PBL unit, students learned how to read nutrition labels and began discussing not only the food options presented in the unit but also some of their favorite snacks. Over several days, different students brought up examples of some of the class favorites, debating how healthy or unhealthy they were and providing evidence from the nutrition labels. The students' focus on the nutritional value of what they indulged in not only helped to contribute to the learning outcomes of the PBL unit but also made the students keenly aware of what they were eating.

Problem Definition

Because PBL units are designed around an ill-structured problem and students do not initially receive all of the information, some research needs to be conducted before students can define the problem they are facing. This phase, called Problem Definition, is when students are introduced to the idea that solving a real-world problem consists of two components: understanding the issue and knowing the constraints. The students have to work together to discuss the issue they are facing and then analyze the constraints or limitations that are associated with it. The constraints are the defining feature of a problem. If there are no limitations, then you are working on a project, not a problem.

In the PBL unit in which students are members of a web design team, students come to understand that the issue is how to create a website that not only educates and persuades but also connects possible donors to a specific issue. The constraints for this problem include the need for the website to attract financial donors, the quick turnaround time the team has to create a mockup, and the best language to use to embody the message of the client.

During this phase, students need to collaborate to create a specific problem definition for the unit, keeping the following format in mind: *How will we (issue) taking into account (constraints)?*

Once the class has reached a consensus on the problem definition, this then guides their next steps in the unit. In the unit where students are members of a web design team, the problem definition might look like this: *How will we attract the most donations keeping in mind that we want to use language that empowers the recipients?*

Problem Resolution

In the Problem Resolution phase of a problem-based learning unit, students work together to decide on the content they want to include in their final presentation or product. Remember, the final task in each PBL unit is different. For the examples noted earlier in this chapter, students may create a website mockup or provide recommendations for a television commercial for a presidential candidate. Students use their problem definition as a springboard to find resolutions for the problem narrative. During this phase, students divide the workload and assign tasks as needed to complete the product.

In one PBL unit, students explore the difference between graffiti and street art by playing the stakeholder role of members of a youth center council who have the opportunity to argue for the installation of a graffiti park at the youth center. My favorite presentations have come from this unit as students cite reasons that a graffiti park may be valuable to the community. Their colorful presentations spotlight examples from around the US and allow students to connect the creation of art to building relationships with communities, social responsibility, and appreciation for the arts in general.

If the Problem Resolution phase takes the form of a presentation, students also need to deliver the presentation effectively. This part of the PBL unit develops organizational and communication skills as students decide on the best way to persuade their audience and present their ideas clearly.

Problem Debrief

In this final part of a PBL unit, students have the chance to reflect on the different perspectives involved in the problem they just completed. They may revisit content where there were questions and guest speakers may be invited into class. Students may connect their learning to other related topics. The PBL unit often concludes with a debriefing activity designed to get students thinking about the problem-solving process and what they learned during the unit. This last activity allows students to make connections between the unit itself and the world around them.

References

Collins, A., & Kapur, M. (2015). Cognitive apprenticeship. In R. K. Sawyer (Ed.), *The Cambridge handbook of the learning sciences* (2nd ed., pp. 109–127). Cambridge University Press.

Horak, A. K. (2013). *The effect of using problem-based learning in middle school gifted science classes on student achievement and students' perceptions of classroom quality* (Order No. 3591082). Available from ProQuest Dissertations & Theses Global. (1433825100).

Stepien, W. J., & Pyke, S. L. (1997). Designing problem-based learning units. *Journal for the Education of the Gifted, 20*(4), 380–400.

Chapter 3

The Case for Using Problem-Based Learning

Kimberley Daly

PBL as a Vehicle to Leverage Curiosity

When students engage in a PBL unit, they immerse themselves in a problem that takes them out of the traditional role of a student listening and learning from a teacher. Collaboratively, with their teacher, students are now web designers, media consultants, members of a youth center council, or in some other role working through a problem narrative that is connected to a real-world issue.

Problem-based learning capitalizes on students' natural curiosity. Units are structured so that students acquire content knowledge while they work through solving the problem. Many PBL units are also transdisciplinary; students may be members of an English language arts class but the PBL unit's subject matter crosses into social studies and mathematics too. While students continue to develop reading, writing, research, and oral skills, they may also be practicing

 DOI: 10.4324/9781003452461-5

data analysis, synthesizing primary/secondary sources, or applying scientific reasoning skills. The PBL unit is not separate from regular classroom instruction. Rather, it is perfectly aligned with the skills and standards that students need to be successful on state tests and can be embedded within the regular scope and sequence of the school year.

The Difference Between Problem- and Project-Based Learning

When I say PBL to someone who doesn't know a lot about the work we do, they often confuse problem-based learning with project-based learning. Although both problem-based learning and project-based learning engage students in activities that promote critical thinking and problem-solving, they are not the same. Both pedagogical methods fall under the umbrella of inquiry-based instruction. While problem-based learning is based around an ill-structured problem and focuses on self-directed inquiry to inform decision-making, project-based learning is defined by a structured project for students to complete accompanied by teacher-directed instruction to provide the content knowledge.

The ill-structured problem in problem-based learning allows students to connect within and between disciplines and to their lived experiences. It also provides an opening for student questions to drive learning. This helps students to formulate deeper reasoning and build critical thinking skills.

Another defining feature of problem-based learning is that students make meaning by analyzing multiple perspectives throughout the course of the problem narrative. If the teacher is teaching multiple sections of a given subject, it is possible that the sequence of objectives addressed in the problem narrative will unfold slightly differently in

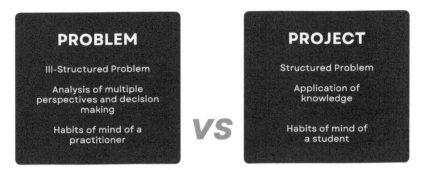

Figure 3.1 Problem- vs. project-based learning.
Project ExCEL-Ignite | Letterpress Communications

each class session. In this way, PBL pushes students to understand the complexity of knowledge and supports the development of analytical reasoning and self-direction. In project-based learning, the focus is on applying knowledge. Students learn through the application of that knowledge.

The last major difference between problem- and project-based learning is that problem-based learning develops the habits of mind of the practitioner while project-based learning continues to develop the habits of mind of the students. Remember, in problem-based learning, the teacher and students are both in the stakeholder role. Both share ownership of the problem and have the authority to make decisions. This helps students to develop skills and abilities that build their capacity and efficacy, like self-direction. These are the same skills they will need later in the workplace or higher education. In project-based learning, teachers are more likely to be instructors who provide better ways to achieve the desired final product (Savery, 2006) and instruction may be provided according to specific learning needs.

Constructivism

Problem- and project-based learning are both forms of constructivist pedagogy. Constructivism (Bruner, 1962; Vygotsky, 1978) is a learning theory whereby individuals create new understandings through problem-solving. Constructivism also stresses that learning is a social activity; that is, something that people do together in collaboration with each other. In problem-based learning, these collaborative activities could include identifying what is known and putting it on the Learning Issues Board, conducting research, discussing different points of view, or creating a presentation. Collaboration is between the students and teacher together as equals in the stakeholder role.

In project-based learning, students also do research but most of the activity is focused on getting to the final product and correct answer. The teacher needs to first deliver the instruction necessary for students to engage in the project-based learning activity and then also provide the technical support necessary for students to complete their work. This may mean providing materials, computers, or other resources. It may also require the teacher to provide scaffolding for students who need extra support.

How Good, Challenging Curriculum Can Help Teachers to Enact Educational Change

Enacting educational change is not easy. Sustaining educational change is even harder. But even as I write this, I know wholeheartedly that good, challenging curriculum accompanied by focused, sustained professional learning and ongoing support can help teachers to enact real educational change in the classroom.

I know because I've seen it firsthand.

Over the course of my career, I have been handed curriculum that I was expected to teach. I have also led many professional learning sessions. I stood where many of you stand now- with a roster of over 100 students, teaching a subject where administrators worry about achieving passing scores on state standardized assessments. I have taught students who lived in poverty, were recent immigrants, or were multilingual learners. Some of my students had special educational needs and my classes also had gifted students.

I've also groaned and rolled my eyes the same exact way some of you have done when the next, newest, or greatest thing was introduced to you.

But what I've also learned over the years is the following: those who initiate and adopt curriculum or pedagogical practice never have bad intentions. The administrators and instructional designers who previously told me that structural analysis, leveled literacy intervention, the science of reading, or anything else generally had the best intentions for students. They wanted to improve student outcomes and assist students who were struggling. They wanted to make teachers aware of new and best practice for the classroom. Unfortunately, many good ideas, including those backed by substantial research regarding student outcomes, do not get the proper funding or follow-through they really require.

The Case for Problem-Based Learning

The most striking thing I have noticed about problem-based learning and the work we do is that the PBL curriculum we develop and use contains so much more than just the problem narrative that the students and teacher are collaboratively working through. The curriculum is designed in such a way that students are not only developing content skills but also practicing skills that will be beneficial for them later in life. They are asked to draw on other disciplines, as well as their own experiences.

Transdisciplinarity

The problem-based learning unit may initially be focused on a topic that, on the surface, appears to be geared toward English language arts, history, or science. However, as students progress through the PBL unit and come up with relevant questions, it is very possible that they will cross disciplinary boundaries. It is common for PBL units to be transdisciplinary, meaning the PBL unit requires students to integrate and synthesize information from the humanities, mathematics, and/or the sciences, thereby pushing them past traditional boundaries (Leavy, 2011). Working across subjects, making connections, and transferring and applying information is a good thing and helps students to learn how to process information in different ways and for different purposes. In life, we cross subjects all the time, processing different bits of information to work and live. Even everyday tasks, such as baking a cake, require us to engage with multiple disciplines. Reading a recipe requires skills from English language. Measuring flour, water, and other ingredients requires mathematical skills. And baking the cake correctly in the oven at the correct temperature requires some understanding of science. If we misread the recipe, measure an ingredient incorrectly, or bake the cake for too long, our cake will most likely not be a sweet treat and we'll have to start again.

The real-world problems presented in PBL require students to connect to other disciplines. It helps students to see that content areas aren't divided into 45-minute periods or 90-minute blocks. For example, in a PBL unit for an English language arts class where students are in the stakeholder role of community organization workers aiming to preserve honeybees by installing apiaries in urban settings, students may come into the unit not really understanding the issue of why pollinators are important. This question may lead them to investigate how honeybees contribute to the ecosystem, crossing into science. This transdisciplinary exploration and eventual understanding of the honeybee issue will help students to move forward in the PBL unit, school, and life.

In another PBL unit, students are in the stakeholder role of members of an enviro-education team for a nonprofit organization. The team submitted a presentation proposal for an upcoming festival and the education coordinator recently received word that this proposal has advanced to the final selection round. The team still has work to do to create a more focused proposal and presentation. When students start the PBL unit, they most likely have very little understanding of how plastic can be recycled, with the exception of what they see in their own neighborhoods. The writing and reading skills needed to create the proposal and presentation are generally taught in English language arts classes, but students also need to explore plastic pollution, waste, and impacts on other environmental systems, including the

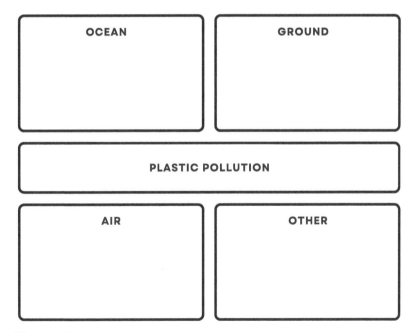

SAMPLE: INTERCONNECTEDNESS GRAPHIC ORGANIZER

The Interconnectedness of Environmental Systems

Each of the plastic management/clean-up solutions has complex ramifications/effects. Use the following graphic organizer to help you see the interconnectedness of each method on various environmental systems.

OCEAN

GROUND

PLASTIC POLLUTION

AIR

OTHER

Figure 3.2 Transdisciplinarity: crossing disciplinary boundaries.

Project ExCEL-Ignite | Letterpress Communications

ocean. Research activities require the students to cross into science and environmental studies as they come to understand how each plastic management method has an effect on the environment. The graphic organizer above is used in the unit to help students to see how clean-up solutions are connected.

Standards-Aligned Education

One of the most frequent questions we receive about the PBL units we develop is whether or not the units are aligned to state standards. This is certainly understandable in the current culture of accountability and standardized testing. When our PBL units are written, our curriculum writer Dana, a middle school English language arts teacher herself, aligns each unit to not only the English language arts standards where we are located (Virginia) but to the US Common Core State Standards (CCSS) for English language arts. Our units are written with American grades 4 to 10 in mind but can be scaffolded up or down for lower or higher grades. The PBL units also contain support for multilingual learners and supplementary materials to give teachers as much background information as possible to the unit's problem narrative and provide options for resources, reflective activities, and extensions.

As we have worked in different states and different subject areas over time, we have aligned some units with other state standards for English language arts and social studies, as well as the International Baccalaureate Middle Years Programme (IBMYP). Additionally, current PBL units have been aligned to the Next Generation Science Standards (NGSS). The alignment of units with standards helps teachers to see that problem-based learning is not a standalone activity. Units can be easily integrated into a program of studies and meet student learning objectives. A PBL unit helps students to develop the skills necessary for state standardized assessments. After our teachers familiarize themselves with the units and have a chance to implement one, they find that they have good value for the time spent on them.

When I fully understood everything PBL could accomplish and how much of an impact it could have on the lives of teachers and students, I was not surprised when Anne was suspected of wanting to initiate a curriculum coup. The units engage students in a problem that develops critical thinking, conceptual reasoning, reading, writing, and research skills. The units check the boxes for good and challenging curriculum too.

Student-Driven Learning

One of the goals of PBL is for students to develop self-directed learning skills. This means that students have input about what, how, and when they learn. Yes, I know. Some of you are shaking your heads because that sounds impossible. But really, it works. The storyline of a PBL unit is ill-structured. Students and the teacher are in cognitive apprenticeship together. Students are coached by the teacher to develop research questions, plan a course of action, and approach the problem from the position of the stakeholder role. But students decide when, how, and what they will learn during the course of the unit, based on the questions and insights they develop together. In PBL, students develop the habits of mind of professionals as they set goals and timelines, practice problem-solving, and develop the skills needed to be successful.

Gail (not her real name), a seventh-grade teacher, explained the difference between teacher-driven instruction and student-driven PBL instruction as follows:

> Non-PBL instruction is when I'm doing direct instruction and students are independently practicing. In PBL, it didn't work that way and there was a difference. They [the students] came in and they had their meeting and then they started delegating.

When students are self-directed in their learning and the PBL unit is student-driven, students overall share a greater sense of ownership in the unit and have higher levels of engagement and motivation.

An Even Playing Field

One of the most interesting things about our PBL curriculum is that it puts all students on an even playing field. At the beginning of a PBL unit, *every* student in the class – students with reading difficulties, on-level students, multilingual learners, and gifted/advanced students – all have gaps in their knowledge. This is by design. The ill-structured problem presented at the start of the unit provides some information while leaving other information out. Every student paying attention will have questions because there are gaps. The class becomes a safe space not to know something. It is amazing to see how this allows students to emerge. Cooperatively, students work together to find and synthesize information, problem-solve, and create the requested product.

The teacher's role in a PBL unit is to support students as they go through the process of discovery. This means that the teacher pushes students to understand the limits of their knowledge. A teacher may help students to identify and prioritize action steps or find resources but the teacher needs to be careful to stay in the same stakeholder role as the students even though they, of course, are aware of additional information. Cognitive apprenticeship focuses on teaching students complex thinking processes and teachers achieve this through modeling, coaching, and reflection. One teacher I observed, Heidi, was amazing at turning questions back on her students. As the class discussed information on the Learning Issues Board, she was steadfast in not responding to questions with a simple yes or no. She always pushed students to either answer the question themselves or engage with other students to find a way forward. Of course, she knew the answer and could tell them, but she stayed in the stakeholder role intentionally to put responsibility on the students to decide how to learn. Her persistence in this regard ultimately taught the students skills that helped them to stand on their own in other classes too.

Heidi's success with her students also showed the strong relationships she had developed with them. During PBL, instead of students becoming frustrated at her lack of answers to their questions, they enthusiastically engaged in the process and searched for ways to move forward.

21st-Century Skills and Future-Ready Students

Depending on your school district, you may also be familiar with 21st-century skills or preparing future-ready students. Both are connected to the idea of ensuring that every student is prepared for a future that requires more analytical thinking, collaboration, and advanced communication skills. Although there are different approaches to 21st-century skills, many frameworks focus on cognitive skills, intra- and inter-personal skills, and technical skills (Pellegrino, 2017).

Commonly, these are the skills that show up in 21st-century and future-ready frameworks:

- ◈ Critical thinking;
- ◈ Creativity;
- ◈ Collaboration;
- ◈ Communication; and
- ◈ Information literacy skills.

In PBL units, students build the above skills as they navigate through the unit's problem. As students begin a unit by learning their stakeholder role, the opening problem narrative presents students with some information but leaves some with gaps. By using the Learning Issues Board, students can document what they know and develop questions for further investigation. This process develops critical thinking and collaboration skills. In a PBL unit in which students are media consultants working on a presidential campaign, they have to look at candidates through the lens of foreign policy. Students collaborate to sift through transcripts, documents, and videos related to a specific event. This builds information literacy and critical thinking skills. Students also need to come to a consensus about which candidate is stronger concerning their handling of the situation.

SAMPLE: PROFIT COMPARISON CHART

Food for Thought | Profits

Imagine it. You are on the concessions committee and need to evaluate which items to sell this year. Examine the concession stand profit reports from the last two football seasons provided by your instructor. Then complete the chart and answer the questions below.

PIZZA

Year 1 Profit _____
Year 2 Profit _____

Circle One - From Year 1 to Year 2, did pizza profits:

INCREASE or DECREASE
By how much?

_____

CANDY

Year 1 Profit _____
Year 2 Profit _____

Circle One - From Year 1 to Year 2, did candy profits:

INCREASE or DECREASE
By how much?

_____

CHIPS & SNACKS

Year 1 Profit _____
Year 2 Profit _____

Circle One - From Year 1 to Year 2, did snacks profits:

INCREASE or DECREASE
By how much?

_____

DRINKS

Year 1 Profit _____
Year 2 Profit _____

Circle One - From Year 1 to Year 2, did drink profits:

INCREASE or DECREASE
By how much?

_____

Which category of items saw the **biggest increase** in profits?
Which category of items saw the **biggest decrease** in profits?
Which item(s) appear to be **growing** in popularity?
Which item(s) appear to be **declining** in popularity?

Figure 3.3 21st-century skills: critical thinking and informational literacy.

As students conduct research and find information to answer their questions, they have to reflect on their learning and listen to other, perhaps opposing, points of view. The interpersonal skill of effective communication is supported by the cognitive skills used to process information to formulate appropriate, and often creative, responses.

The problem-based learning unit also presents many opportunities for students to develop and improve informational literacy. Some units may present students with the opportunity to locate, compare, and analyze data while other units may ask students to evaluate the validity of media sources. The units provide students with multiple opportunities for sustained practice in determining an author's purpose, evaluating sources, and analyzing techniques used to construct arguments, all of which are skills students need to be future-ready and for state standardized assessments.

In one unit in which students are members of a concession stand committee for a high school booster club, they need to look at how different types of food impact the money they raise. Students are presented with data concerning the concession stand offerings for two years and the profits from selling them. As they process the data, students develop informational literacy, critical thinking, and communication skills while sorting through how different food items have been more or less profitable. The activity below helps students to process the data they uncover during this unit.

Global Competence and Global Citizenship

Over the last few decades, as the awareness of globalization has increased, educators and administrators have come to realize the value of developing global competence skills in students and fostering students to become engaged global citizens (Daly et al., 2022). Global citizenship education has a long history and educators now weave global competence and global citizenship lessons into core subjects, combining the development of content skills with communication skills, critical thinking, and respect for other perspectives.

When I was a P-12 teacher and taught International Baccalaureate (IB) coursework, I appreciated the IB's overarching commitment to developing students' international-mindedness. This focus on understanding ourselves by connecting with others and recognizing others' perspectives and cultures was apparent in core subjects and electives. Students were prepared to be part of a global community and sustained inquiry around larger, global topics led to exploration, reflection, and, sometimes, action. Our PBL units can also be used to develop global competence and global citizenship skills as students learn to appreciate the interconnectedness of local, national, and global topics.

To provide an example of this, in a PBL unit in which students are members of a web development team competing for the opportunity to develop a website focused on raising money to support girls' education equality, students learn how important education is for not only one girl but also her community and the world. They complete an activity called Spheres of Influence, in which they organize what they have uncovered.

Additionally, problem-based learning units help students to develop global competence and global citizenship skills by facilitating student self-directed learning. During a PBL unit, the whole class works together to define, understand, and resolve the presented problem. Students have opportunities to practice critical thinking skills, evaluate a wide range of points of view, and consider responsible action at local and global levels. Several of the units we have developed also offer opportunities for students to think about their role in shared humanity and can be connected to the United Nations Sustainable Development Goals (SDGs).

The main reason that PBL fits in well with developing global competence and global citizenship is because of the real-world problems presented in the problem narratives. The real-world problem relies on students recognizing how disciplines are interrelated. When students engage in a PBL unit, they continue to develop reading, writing, collaboration, and speaking skills. They advocate for positions and develop

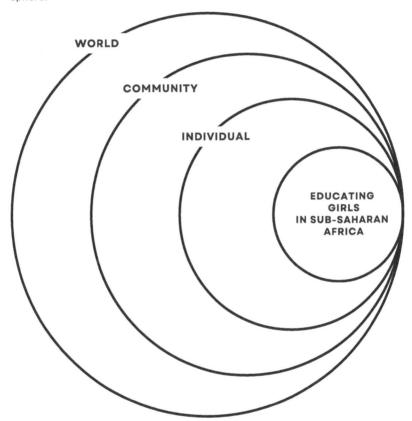

SAMPLE: SPHERES OF INFLUENCE

The Power of Education

Think about all that you know about the power of education for girls in Sub-Saharan Africa. Fill in the chart below to show how education influences each sphere.

WORLD

COMMUNITY

INDIVIDUAL

EDUCATING GIRLS IN SUB-SAHARAN AFRICA

Figure 3.4 Global competence and citizenship: spheres of influence.

Project ExCEL-Ignite | Letterpress Communications

plans for solutions. All of these activities help students to become engaged global citizens.

Another reason PBL can work as a vehicle to develop global competence and global citizenship skills is because of its focus on problem-solving. Every unit puts students in a stakeholder role in which they need to solve a problem and complete a specific task. Students focus on making connections and developing skills that are found across many different subjects. This knowledge transfers and can be applied across various contexts.

Talent-Spotting

In terms of educational change, one of the most exciting things about PBL is the potential for it to be used for talent-spotting. As Anne mentioned in the introduction, gifted programs have a long history of underrepresentation. Other teachers I have worked with over the last several years have noted this as well, explaining that district policies identify students at the elementary level, often through testing, and stop there. Although some districts allow for special requests, teacher recommendations, or identification when students move into a district, testing is still the norm.

But in the ExCEL Model (our model), PBL is effectively used as a universal screening method that embeds a dynamic performance assessment into the problem narrative. Our model is a process and includes a systemic approach that is design-based and focuses on continuous improvement. Using the observational model created by Shaklee (1993) and the categories of attributes of gifted learners developed by Shaklee et al. (1997), PBL supports talent-spotting because it provides teachers with the opportunity to observe student performance that is unlikely to occur during traditional, teacher-driven instruction. As a part of our work with problem-based learning, this model was revised for use with general education teachers (Shaklee & Horak, 2014) and is included with the professional learning we provide to teachers.

In the EAEP observational model, the attributes of gifted learners are grouped into four categories:

- ❖   Exceptional Learner;
- ❖   Exceptional User;
- ❖   Exceptional Generator; and
- ❖   Exceptional Motivation.

Attributes in Action
Traits and Identifiers in the Middle School PBL Classroom

Exceptional Learner

Associated with the ability to acquire, understand, and retain information.

Look for students who demonstrate patterns of:

- Attention to/knowledge of detail.
- Understanding other perspectives.
- Inquisitiveness, asking extended questions.
- Recalling past experiences.
- Transferring information between experiences.
- Intrinsic motivation.
- Stepping up or "leaning into" the problem.

Exceptional User

Associated with the ability to apply information, especially to problem-solve, reason, or transform knowledge between symbol systems.

Look for students who demonstrate patterns of:

- Incorporating details into writing and drawings.
- Asking questions that integrate different perspectives.
- Flexibility in thinking.
- Experimenting with knowledge.
- Using interesting words.
- Manipulating symbol systems (words, dance, art, music, numbers) to demonstrate knowledge.

Exceptional Generator

Associated with the ability to be creative, curious, humorous, self-expressive, and non-conforming.

Look for students who demonstrate patterns of:

- Risk-taking.
- Open-mindedness.
- Humor.
- Independent thinking.
- Reflection.
- Asking unusual or unexpected questions that move thinking forward.

Exceptional Motivator

Associated with the ability to self-initiate, lead peers, and focus intensely on a topic of interest.

Look for students who demonstrate patterns of:

- Intense engagement or interest.
- Taking on the stakeholder role.
- Taking the lead in discussions and group work.
- Taking on new roles or responsibilities.
- Speaking up more frequently.
- Persuading, encouraging, or motivating peers.

Figure 3.5 Attributes in action: traits and identifiers in the middle school classroom.

Project ExCEL-Ignite | Letterpress Communications

Along with a definition, each category also breaks down the qualities and behaviors a teacher may observe in students during a PBL unit. Teachers can note observations throughout the course of the unit and then later make holistic recommendations, grounded by data, for students in whom they see behaviors within the context of talent and potential. These recommendations are different from traditional teacher rating scales as students are all observed using the same pedagogical method: PBL. Teachers also receive ongoing support throughout this process.

It is always exciting for us to hear from teachers about what they observe in their classes. Ava, a seventh-grade teacher, was teaching a PBL unit in which students were in the stakeholder role of members of a parks and recreation department planning the redevelopment of an abandoned lot into a soccer field. She told us about one particular student, Sarah, who was very curious and did a lot of additional research on her own. As with teacher names, I have changed student names to protect confidentiality. Ava said:

> Sarah went out to further her knowledge about gentrification and she even brought things back to class. She was very invested in it and asked questions, and she gave counter arguments. …It was something that she could immediately identify with in her neighborhood and perhaps she knew other people who had been in that situation. I think because it was real life it was relatable and she could connect with it.

Another middle school teacher, Heather, taught the same PBL unit and had an interesting experience with a generally introverted student named André. She explained:

> This student is extremely quiet, introverted. I'll even say anxious. In the past, he demonstrated this need to be perfect, this need to just have it right. He often takes his time because he doesn't want to sacrifice the standard of his work. But there was [sic] some

times in which he would have his hand up and he would keep it up even while other people were raising their hands in order to be heard, which I really liked because he valued what he had to say enough that he kept his hand up. He took a risk because he's very shy. I make a point now of really watching him.

The behaviors these teachers observed may not have been noticed outside of the PBL unit, during traditional teacher-driven instruction, or without specific professional learning about the observational model. Both students were identified by their teachers using our talent-spotting model.

References

Bruner, J. (1962). *On knowing: Essays for the left hand.* Harvard University Press.

Daly, K., Myers, L., Horak, A. K., & Plowden, D. L. (2022). Developing global citizenship education skills and understanding through deliberate pedagogical choices. In S. Lillo Kang & S. McIntosh (Eds.), *Enacting equitable global citizenship education in schools: Lessons from dialogue between research and practice.* Rowman & Littlefield Publishers.

Leavy, P. (2011). *Essentials of transdisciplinary research: Using problem centered methodologies.* Left Coast Press, Inc.

Pellegrino, J. (2017). Teaching, learning and assessing 21st century skills. In S. Guerriero (Ed.), *Pedagogical knowledge and the changing nature of the teaching profession* (pp. 223–251), OECD Publishing. https://doi.org/10.1787/9789264270695-12-en

Savery, J. R. (2006). Overview of problem-based learning: Definitions and distinctions. *Interdisciplinary Journal of Problem-Based Learning, 1*(1). https://doi.org/10.7771/1541-5015.1002

Shaklee, B. (1993). Preliminary findings of the early assessment for exceptional potential project. *Roeper Review*, *16*(2), 105–109. https://doi.org/10.1080/02783199309553551

Shaklee, B., Barbour, N., Ambrose, R., & Hansford, S. (1997). *Designing and using portfolios*. Allyn and Bacon.

Shaklee, B., & Horak, A. K. (2014). *Project ExCEL*. U.S. Department of Education, Institute of Educational Sciences, Javits Gifted and Talented Students Education Grant Program.

Vygotsky, L. S. (1978). *Mind in society: The development of higher psychological processes*. Harvard University Press.

Chapter 4

Problem-Based Learning as a Means for Educational Change

Kimberley Daly

The **GOAT** of Instruction

Good, challenging curriculum can certainly be a vehicle for educational change. In the age of accountability, we understand that alignment with standards is extremely important for teachers, administrators, and schools. PBL curriculum is aligned with standards to help teachers and administrators to see the connections. But what we have found is that PBL offers so much more in terms of changing the climate of schools and classrooms and the lives of students. Yes, teachers can connect the material in PBL units to what is on standardized tests and students are able to practice necessary skills during the PBL unit. But this is not traditional instruction. The classroom is not silent but full of language and literacy. Students are immersed in an engaging, real-world storyline that is transdisciplinary and allows students to connect to topics personally.

 DOI: 10.4324/9781003452461-6

One thing I have heard repeatedly while working with teachers is that once they try a PBL unit, they want to teach them all the time. Teachers immediately see that they can cover required content within a PBL unit and they love how engaged students are during the narrative.

Problem-based learning is student-driven and promotes active learning with the teacher and students in cognitive apprenticeship together. At the beginning, everyone starts at the same point, with the same gaps in knowledge, and needing to work together. Student curiosity, leadership, and advocacy are showcased as students progress through the PBL unit.

Problem-based learning also can be used as a vehicle for talent-spotting. Our PBL units have been used as a universal screening method with a dynamic performance assessment to find and identify potential. The implementation of PBL along with talent-spotting has proven effective in narrowing gaps in identification and providing access to advanced courses. This is especially important for closing gaps for students who have traditionally been underrepresented in gifted and advanced coursework, including Black and Latinx students, economically disadvantaged students, multilingual learners, and students with special educational needs.

Finally, PBL offers not only content instruction but the development of 21st-century and global citizenship skills. These skills are necessary in every subject and are also important for students to compete and be successful in the global community.

PBL in Action

For the last several years, my work has centered on the implementation of problem-based learning in schools. Bringing on any new initiative is not always easy; it requires buy-in from school districts, central office personnel, principals, and teachers and it often takes time to develop relationships with new school districts to enable successful implementation. That said, once relationships are developed and the groundwork is established, I have seen real change happen in classrooms and schools. Student achievement has improved and teachers have changed their perceptions of student potential and recommended more students for advanced classes. Teachers have become PBL cheerleaders and pushed for the expanded use of PBL units in the classroom. We have seen these positive outcomes be energizing for students, teachers, and schools.

Increasing Representation in Gifted and Advanced Classes

Because of the funding we receive, we focus our work in schools with populations of culturally, linguistically, and economically diverse students. These are schools that are typically already burdened with the most intense interventions and support requirements. Often, at the leadership level, there is a well-intended inclination to shield schools in these circumstances and, consequently, their teachers and students.

It is understandable, but misguided. This grossly underestimates teachers. It sells students short too. So, we ask to talk to the teachers. Time and time again, the teachers we talk to recognize what we are doing as something that aligns with their core beliefs and something they want to do.

Before teachers even begin teaching PBL units, they are provided with professional learning that immerses them in a problem narrative. They are immersed in the stakeholder role and experience many of the same emotions that their students will eventually experience in the classroom during a PBL curriculum unit. Teachers have to sort information, determine what they know, and decide on a plan of action. They don't know everything and they learn together.

For one district, this was the moment that got them hooked. Representatives from an urban school district, including gifted coordinators and teachers, were invited to experience one of our professional learning sessions dedicated to problem-based learning. They liked how the participants were fully engaged and were eager to bring PBL to their district. The gifted coordinator continued to stay in touch with Anne. When we applied for additional funding, the school district came on as an implementation partner. Problem-based learning was embraced as a way to identify more students for Gifted and Talented classes in middle school.

The majority of the teachers we work with have not only taught exclusively during an age of accountability focused on competencies and testing but also attended school themselves in that era as well. As a result, we have learned that there is a learning curve with PBL. It is not uncommon to hear comments doubting that students can handle autonomy and make decisions in the classroom. One teacher expressed concern that middle school students were not mature enough to make appropriate decisions about their learning path. There are also fears expressed about classroom management. During professional learning, we often start with reassurance and an acknowledgment that it is okay to be anxious about something new. We explain that facilitating PBL is not done perfectly the first time. It takes time.

In the case of the school district that I mentioned above, the fears and anxiety were no different. But even with the initial uneasiness, teachers left their first professional learning session excited to teach PBL units. When they saw the curriculum and the resources available, they immediately recognized the possibilities for their students.

Months later, after the teachers had taught their first PBL unit and used the EAEP model to identify students, their enthusiasm came through when explaining to me what they saw in class. One teacher, Barbara, discussed Mateo and his ability to ask thoughtful questions that pushed others to think more deeply:

> Throughout the time we were working on this, he was able to push the conversation by answering questions in a thoughtful manner. He'd listen and then come up with the most amazing ideas. Other students would react to what he said and it moved a lot of the discussion where it really needed to go.

Another teacher, Monica, was really struck by how differently a student named Cora behaved during PBL as opposed to non-PBL class instruction. Monica described how the student usually is in class outside of PBL, "In class, she lacks with everything…And she doesn't participate as much. She's one of the students that you get frustrated with, because you want her to do her work."

For both students, PBL brought out behaviors that were strikingly different from when the students were involved in teacher-driven activities. Mateo's questions drove other students to develop more depth to their responses. Cora's academic behavior changed completely due to her engagement with PBL.

Because the PBL unit brought out a completely different side of Cora, Monica identified her using the EAEP model. She explained:

I feel like she [Cora] really liked the flexibility of the thinking. She was experimenting. She really led a lot of discussion…and she took that self-initiative to kind of stand out and lead and get done what needed to get done. When I brought the leaders together specifically, she really kind of rallied with them and made sure the presentation was what it needed to be. I saw a whole different side of her with her motivation to just participate and learn, and lead and speak up more than I had ever seen throughout the school year with her.

The qualities Barbara noted – flexible thinking, leadership, intense interest, and intrinsic motivation – most likely contributed to her identifying Cora. She saw a spark in Cora that she hadn't seen before. She saw potential.

In addition to the above, the teachers described how previously silent students spoke up during PBL and how some students connected and engaged with the material. Ben was one of those students. Barbara elaborated:

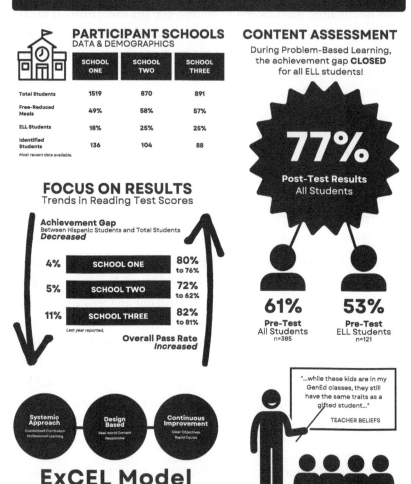

Figure 4.1 Closing learning and equity gaps with Project ExCEL.

Project ExCEL-Ignite | Letterpress Communications

He [Ben] first comes off [as] kind of calm, cool, and collected. He didn't want to really stand out. He just wanted to be one of the cool guys that doesn't really speak up a lot. But you could tell that he wanted to because he was interested in it. I could see that he wanted to do more and learn more and speak up more.

The district continues with PBL implementation and we continue to provide professional learning and ongoing support to teachers. Teachers love the units they teach because they see their students bloom as learners and thinkers. Students are curious and engaged. Our schools are building momentum and working with us to ensure sustainability. As time goes on and as teachers implement more PBL units, they will develop their expertise as PBL facilitators and become more skilled in observing talent according to the EAEP model. The district will continue to decrease the gaps in representation in gifted classes.

Improving Student Achievement

Principals and teachers often choose problem-based learning because of its potential to improve student achievement. But it's really a whole package. Problem-based learning curriculum can be used as a universal screening method with a dynamic performance assessment for talent-spotting. It develops standards-aligned content skills and offers opportunities for students to build creative and critical thinking, problem-solving, reflection, and global competence skills. It promotes student-driven learning. And it gets teachers excited about teaching. That's a lot of bang for the buck.

This was exactly the case for one suburban school district. Problem-based learning offers many benefits to schools and students. Adriana, a principal in an often-underperforming school, explained why she adopted PBL:

I was trying to look for instructional models that would help us to perhaps change or find a different way of teaching…the PBL model was one of the things that I wanted to adopt to see what the results would be, what the level of engagement would be for the kids.

After implementation in her school, feedback was positive and Adriana was extremely pleased with the results. About what she witnessed in classrooms, she said:

It [PBL] provides students the opportunity to really learn based on the modality that they learn best… I had the opportunity to go in and see the kids working. It wasn't that everybody was doing the same thing at the same time, but all the kids were engaged. They were asking questions, engaged in the writing or the research, and I did enjoy that.

Teachers also saw how PBL made an impact on the students. An eighth-grade teacher, Paige, said:

They [the students] were more able to consider other peoples' opinions and different things that happen outside of their little world. They were able to agree and disagree and do it without that bickering that they normally get into over nothing. It [PBL] taught them how to appreciate each other more.

The arc of the PBL narrative requires everyone in class, i.e., the teacher and students, to be in the same stakeholder role. They must work together to complete the task required by the unit.

Another teacher, Stacie, noted the interactive way that understanding and working with informational texts was developed through the PBL units. After explaining how she had to make sure the standards were covered in her school, she elaborated:

Kids in middle school struggle the most with informational texts. They will pick fiction above them. This was an opportunity to teach informational texts and primary versus secondary texts at such a deeper, higher level. Most importantly, it's fun for them.

Informational text is included in most English language arts standards and working with primary and secondary sources is included in many social studies standards. Teachers soon come to realize that PBL units provide students with the necessary practice to meet state standards but are also engaging.

And talent-spotting is not forgotten. The same district did not lose sight of the fact that our PBL curriculum could also be used to identify potential in students and make recommendations for placement in gifted and advanced classes. Several teachers who taught PBL units told me stories of students who often did not score highly on district or state standardized testing but were highly engaged and demonstrated attributes of gifted potential according to the EAEP model.

Catherine told me about a 7th grader named Tamara.

Before problem-based learning, Tamara often didn't come to school. She had a lot of difficulties at home and when she was in class, she was rarely engaged. When Tamara was asked to take notes about a particular topic, she often wrote a note to a friend. Past standardized testing showed that she read below grade level.

But with PBL, there was a complete shift in Tamara. Catherine described her transformation:

> It's hard to say what exactly clicked with her...She asked to sit in front on the second day. This is a girl that never really engaged with any of her classmates before. She was engaging with her classmates, she was doing the research, she was doing everything I asked her to do, she had not one day where she dozed off in class. She was just absolutely in love with this unit.

In addition to Tamara's engagement level, her grades also improved.

Widespread Implementation

Given the benefits of PBL for students and schools, our evidence shows the potential for PBL curriculum to be used to increase student achievement and close equity gaps. But widespread implementation still eludes us. One barrier is the need for education. While many teachers have a working knowledge of what they consider to be PBL curriculum, they might have had little opportunity to learn the pedagogy connected to it during their pre-service training. Another barrier to widespread PBL implementation is access to effective curriculum-aligned professional learning (PL). This type of professional learning marks a shift away from traditional models because it is aligned with the curriculum that teachers will use and requires instructional materials to be paired with specific strategies and involves repeated sessions, feedback, and opportunities for reflection (Thomas et al., 2009).

For PBL to be implemented effectively and with fidelity, professional learning is necessary both at the pre-service level and as continuing professional development for in-service teachers. Currently, curriculum-aligned PL is not offered on a comprehensive level and the PL we currently offer is limited by funding, human capacity, and time. This book is an attempt to bridge the gap from the work we have been doing, including professional learning, so that problem-based learning can enjoy more widespread implementation.

Conclusion

Through the work we have done implementing the ExCEL Model during our federally-funded research projects, Anne, Shannon, and I have worked to change teachers' beliefs about students through the PBL curriculum. Students not only develop content, critical thinking, creative, and problem-solving skills but also are empowered to self-direct their learning. Districts and schools can adopt PBL to help to close enrollment gaps in gifted and advanced coursework, as well as provide teachers with a pedagogical approach that meets state standards and develops skills that students need to be successful in an ever-changing and global community.

As Fullan (2016) noted, meaningful educational change takes time. It is a systematic process of initiation, implementation, and continuation that involves developing relationships, short- and long-term planning, and working with a complex network of school and district stakeholders. We have found that once PBL curriculum and adoption is approved, successful implementation is dependent on sustained and focused professional learning with ongoing support.

These are all pieces of a complex puzzle: PBL curriculum, pedagogical practice, and professional learning/support. To enact meaningful change in classrooms and schools and change teachers' beliefs, successful implementation and continuation or sustainability depend on all three pieces fitting together perfectly.

References

Fullan, M. (2016). *The new meaning of educational change* (5th ed.). Teacher's College Press.

Thomas, K., Saucedo, D., & Parker, C. E. (2022). *Transforming K-8 teacher practices through open-educational resources: Unpacking contextual constraints.* SRI International. https://hewlett.org/wp-content/uploads/2023/01/Brief-3-Transforming-Teacher-Practices-OER.pdf

Section 2

Professional Learning with PBL

Chapter 5

Effective Professional Learning

Shannon King

Introduction

I have always loved learning. When I was young, I would sneak into the library to pick out more books than I was allowed. I always returned them. Even now, a new podcast or article will catch my attention and I will find myself engrossed, compelled by the promise of learning something new. I am drawn to people who also love learning. This is how Anne and I, and later Kim, came to work together.

Professional learning, or PL, on the other hand, is another story. I have had a paradoxical relationship with professional learning for educators. Too often, there is no actual learning. Just listening, or perhaps multitasking. That said, most of my career has been related to professional learning for teachers because I believe it is so important to provide educators with effective professional learning support and when professional learning is done right, it can be transformative. One transformative moment for me occurred when I was leading a program in central office supporting best practice in teaching and learning. As

 DOI: 10.4324/9781003452461-8

a part of that work, I attended a PBL training session that Anne was coordinating. It rocked my world. But we will come back to that. In the meantime, let me share how I got there.

Everyone in a School is a Learner

Many educators enter professional learning unhappy. I knew that feeling all too well. My principal asked me to take on the role of instructional coach. At my school, being an instructional coach was a job that meant leading professional learning for an underperforming Title I school. The school was inundated with PL by people who saw it as their job to *fix* everything. Staff and faculty were wary of all professional learning. Even so, I accepted the position.

I did not sleep the night before facilitating my first professional learning day as an instructional coach. I had spent hours planning. On that hot August day, I watched the teachers trudge into the school cafeteria. It was clear that they would rather be setting up their classrooms. My heart sank. I was sure this learning opportunity was doomed. What I had not fully comprehended was this: teachers have so many competing priorities. Professional learning designed for them must be practical. They do not have the time or bandwidth for anything else. Teachers must see a connection to how they can apply what they are learning or they lose interest. Fast. With good reason.

The data dialogue session I was leading that day was a tricky one. It was not immediately applicable and the teachers did not have any data they could work with during the session. On the way out, one veteran teacher said, "You know these learners need support to succeed, too!" while pointing to herself and the other teachers in the room. I know truth when I hear it and that was it. I had not fully comprehended that my teachers were learners too.

From that point on, I have understood that we are all learners in a school. I needed to intentionally include outcomes for teachers in my planning. In whatever way I wanted the students to be taught, I needed to teach teachers in the same way. That is, in a way that respected teachers as adult learners but modeled the experience I wanted them to replicate for their learners. Soon after this insight occurred to me, I found myself experiencing the exact type of professional learning that I was imagining when I found myself in Anne's session on problem-based learning (PBL).

Leading the Learning

After working as an instructional coach, I took a position with Instructional Services, in the same district and office as Anne. Our paths had crossed before when we collaborated on designing a gifted endorsement course. In my role in central office, I was asked to learn more about problem-based learning (PBL). There was interest in the district in using PBL as an avenue to increase the rigor of classroom instruction. It was at that point I found myself in Anne's professional learning session on PBL.

The professional learning embodied all of the things that I had learned were important. Teachers were active participants. The session was designed to engage teachers in a PBL experience. The intention was for them to see and feel what their students would see and feel in a PBL classroom environment. The presenters modeled the experience and then paused to unpack and reflect along the way. Questions were asked and answered. Sometimes questions were answered with questions. At the end, the teachers selected a PBL unit they wanted to implement. Teachers left the session prepared to implement PBL and record videos of themselves during the experience. Later, they returned to engage with the experts in a coaching session, using the videos to support their reflection on their development of the essential skills for facilitating PBL. Essentially, they were metacognitively coached to be a metacognitive coach. As both a learner and a professional development facilitator, it opened my eyes to what professional learning should be.

I was captivated by the compelling nature of the PBL experience. Teachers were focused and attentive. Laptops and personal devices were set aside and ignored. I was gripped by the power of metacognitive coaching to establish and sustain the narrative arc of the problem. I was fascinated by how the PBL facilitator developed and maintained rapport by maintaining the stakeholder role. In PBL, the expert facilitator pulls this off flawlessly, never letting on that they are subtly guiding the direction and flow. They never step out of their role as a member of the stakeholder team, no matter how much the teachers hover above it or try to pull them out of it.

For the teachers participating, it feels as though everything is happening for the first time. Everything is new and happening simultaneously. The teachers see the problem as urgent and important. For the facilitator, it is almost as though the teachers are responding on cue and they can almost predict the next question. The teachers do not know that this is intentional. The PL looks flawless because even though the facilitator knows the content, when a question comes up, they put every question on the Learning Issues Board smoothly, with the same interest, curiosity, and open-mindedness as the teacher asking it.

Sometimes, information suggested during professional learning sessions can also be inaccurate. Or the facilitator may know a particular question would lead in a direction that is unproductive. These also are put on the Learning Issues Board and are worked out by teachers over the course of the PL. No matter what is brought up, the facilitator maintains composure and continues to model curiosity and interest. For the facilitator, it feels like everything is unfolding in a predictable pattern, which is as a result of the intentional design of the ill-structured problem. This intentional approach is tightly aligned with what Darling-Hammond and Cook-Harvey found in their 2018 metanalysis of what works in professional learning.

Sometime after I attended this session, Anne moved to George Mason University, where she had the opportunity expand and develop her work through the Jacob K. Javits Program. When Anne began work on the Javits, she needed a team of experienced professional learning consultants. It spoke to what I believed in and so, I wanted to be a part of it. I was not disappointed. This is when I began working with Kim and Dana. Dana and I continued to work full-time in our other roles and consult on the work related to the Javits while Anne and Kim's efforts were dedicated solely to the grant.

Expanding the Capacity of Educators

To say it is challenging to work in education these days is an understatement. While that is not in question, I would argue it has always been challenging to be in education. A teacher's job encompasses not only teaching but also tending to the well-being of the children entrusted to their care. This is true in districts across the country. The list of things teachers must attend to daily is getting longer and more complex. One of our teachers recently shared with me, "These days I am part-teacher, part-counselor, part-safety inspector, and when I have to craft emails to upset parents, part-lawyer!" This hit home. It reminds me how important it is to support our teachers in taking on the learning of how to implement PBL well while navigating current complexities and balancing competing priorities. Yet, our future and our children are relying on our teachers' success. Giving teachers a professional learning focus, such as PBL, helps to create structure in uncertainty. It paves a pathway for success with manageable steps.

I know why it is so important to provide support to build the capacity of teachers. Educators play a central role in shaping the quality of education and the overall development of students. With our work, this means that in order to teach PBL, teachers need professional learning to support their development and understanding of the effective skills and strategies of a PBL facilitator before they start teaching PBL. They need a research-based, grounded model for observing student performance in a way that will help to identify students with the potential to be successful in advanced classes. They need support in refining and advancing their instructional practice so that PBL instruction and dynamic performance assessment become embedded as a regular part of instruction. And so, the skills required for effective PBL transfer across instructional contexts. Our teachers need support in understanding how to use research-based evidence to advocate for their own growth and engagement, as well as that of their students.

Quality of Education and Student Learning

Before we dive into *how* to provide effective professional learning, let us first explore some of the key reasons *why* it is important to invest in the capacity building of teachers. From lawmakers and politicians to neighbors and relatives, the quality of education is often a concern. It seems to be a no-brainer that we all want to ensure that our students are getting a quality education. We compare the quality of that education from school to school, district to district, and even to schools in other countries.

While we can point to many things that matter, teachers are the primary drivers of education quality (Leu, 2005; Olsen & Wyss, 2022). Well-trained and knowledgeable teachers are more likely to deliver effective instruction, engage students, and create a positive learning environment. High-quality teaching leads to better student outcomes and achievements. And to that end, teachers directly influence student learning and academic performance. When teachers are equipped with the skills, strategies, and resources to implement PBL, they can address diverse learning needs and make learning more effective and inclusive.

Problem-based learning sets teachers up for success in all of these ways. Challenging, PBL curriculum is aligned to state standards and reinforces reading, writing, speaking, and digital literacy skills, in addition to the specific content within the area in which it is taught. Engagement in PBL units helps students to develop collaboration and problem-solving skills, as well as critical thinking strategies. Finally, as many PBL units delve into real-world topics, they also help students to build confidence and motivation in the classroom. These can all translate into higher student achievement and academic performance, as well as a positive classroom environment.

Innovation and Continuous Improvement

More than ever, education is an ever-evolving field. To be effective in the classroom today, teachers must adapt to an educational landscape that is changing at an increasingly dizzying speed. As a result, teaching is a lifelong learning process. Making space for professional learning that is aligned to specific curriculum, like PBL, establishes a culture of continuous improvement. One that makes it safe for teachers to reflect and refine PBL teaching practice.

A continuous improvement approach shrinks the change we are asking of ourselves. It also invites the habits of mind that support a growth mindset (Dweck, 2006). To put this idea into practice, we created and use a rubric to support teachers in making incremental

COGNITIVE APPRENTICESHIP DIMENSIONS

Modeling	Coaching	Scaffolding	Articulation	Reflection	Exploration
Teacher performs a task for student to observe.	Teacher observes students performing a task and facilitates their efforts.	Teacher provides support to help students perform a task.	Teacher encourages students to verbalize their thinking.	Teacher encourages students to examine their own performance.	Teacher invites students to pose and solve their own problems.

Figure 5.1 The dimensions of cognitive apprenticeship.
Adapted from Collins, 2006

changes to their instruction. The Cognitive Apprenticeship Rubric (CAR) was developed to identify the instructional skills that are effective in a PBL environment and differentiate between levels of proficiency (Bland et al., 2018). It focuses on teachers having support to increase their capacity and effectiveness for PBL instruction. The theoretical framework for the CAR draws on educational psychology, curriculum and instruction, and gifted education literature.

After teachers implement a PBL unit, we engage them in a reflection conversation grounded by the rubric. Teachers rate themselves and choose one area of focus for the next round of implementation. We then provide support in the identified area. For example, a teacher may choose responding to questions with questions. Using the rubric to focus teachers on one area helps to narrow change to a manageable scope. Our teachers then focus on the identified area during the next PBL curriculum unit implementation and debrief afterward during another reflection conversation, again grounded by the rubric. Then again, using the rubric, teachers choose another area of focus. The use of the CAR with a focused and reflective approach allows teachers not only to increase their capacity for PBL instruction but tailor their professional growth to their individual contexts and understandings.

Equity and Inclusion

Perhaps the challenge most often shared by the school districts we have worked with across the country is how to help teachers to meet the diverse needs of their student population. And that diversity is growing in many ways, from cultural and linguistic diversity to varying levels of readiness or engagement. That's in addition to making up for the learning loss so often referred to in conversations about education in our post-pandemic world. Effective teacher training emphasizes inclusive teaching practice that supports the diverse needs of students, including those with disabilities, different cultural backgrounds, and varying learning abilities. With our work, we are directly addressing equity and inclusion. It is, in fact, an absolute priority for our federal funding.

Jacob & McGovern (2015) posit that the most important component for teacher growth is to create the conditions for change. The foundations of creating the conditions for change rest on:

◆ Time to develop, absorb, discuss, and practice new knowledge;
◆ Active engagement with curriculum and opportunities to learn in the way they should be teaching students (Opfer & Pedder, 2011); and
◆ Sustained contact hours (Guskey, 1986).

In our professional learning, we create the conditions for change to confront inequity by reflecting on bias, data analysis, and differing perspectives. Teachers' perspective-taking abilities often affect their teaching practice and teachers with more perspective-taking ability may also feel stronger connections to equity or justice goals (Rios et al., 2010). Data analysis is important for informing instruction. Teachers need to be able to deftly and quickly process data presented in various ways. Teachers who can understand and use data can test assumptions, create sound assessments, and influence policy (Mandinach & Gummer, 2016). Reflection involves educators reviewing their teaching and then setting goals and problem-solving (Schön, 1983). Through this process, teachers contribute to creating a more equitable and inclusive education system: one that students want to be a part of because they know they belong there (Gay, 2018; Ladson-Billings, 2021).

Job Satisfaction

Districts are facing critical teacher shortages. Young people are not choosing to pursue teaching as a career and teachers are leaving the profession in droves. And this labor shortage is not going anywhere anytime soon. The 2023 report "No Worker Left Behind" by the nonprofit group America Succeeds describes the significance of how urgent it is to empower people with the skills they need to be successful. For those in education, this means ensuring that teachers have the skills and strategies to implement problem-based learning well.

Professional learning and capacity-building opportunities are key ways of boosting teacher morale and job satisfaction. To optimize these opportunities, we designed our PL differently. Our professional learning program is focused and self-directed. We engage teachers in exactly the way in which they will engage students. They feel competent and equipped to handle challenges. It enhances confidence and overall job performance.

Well-supported teachers stay in the classroom. Teachers reported to us that they stayed in the classroom in lieu of retiring or sought an administrative position because they were excited to take on the growth experience of problem-based learning with the ongoing professional learning support we provided. The teachers we worked with shifted their mindsets away from polemic all or nothing thinking toward a development continuum characterized by growth. Reflection on their instruction with an expert coach, co-teacher, or colleague was crucial. Self-directed growth through collaborative professional learning sustained engagement.

National Development

Finally, professional learning is important because investing in educators' development is ultimately about the greater good. One of the founding beliefs of the US is that a well-educated populace is essential for our country's development. One of our team's core beliefs is that we do this work to make the lives of teachers and students better. By investing in teacher capacity building through professional learning, we can ensure that future generations are equipped with the knowledge and skills needed to contribute to economic, social, and cultural progress. In short, building the capacity of teachers is a strategic investment that has far-reaching benefits for students, schools, communities, and societies at large. It is a critical step toward achieving high-quality, equitable, and effective education systems. It is why we do what we do.

But teacher capacity is often cited by school principals as a perceived obstacle to implementing the project. We typically encounter common misconceptions about teacher capacity. One such misconception is that more years of teaching experience translates to better PBL instruction. The concern being that if the school has a relatively inexperienced teaching staff, implementation will be weak. This leads the principal away from participation. In our work, however, we have found that this is often not the case. Teachers with less experience in the classroom have just as much or even more capacity to facilitate PBL well.

Related to teacher capacity is teacher turnover. If a school has a high turnover, either in any given year or consistently across years, the concern is that it will be too overwhelming for a new teacher to also take on an initiative designed with the depth and complexity of this one. Yet, it is a misconception to think that building teacher capacity is optional, additional, or extra. Given the significance of what building teacher capacity can accomplish, it is essential and should be embedded into the regular routine of teacher practice. We need to build avenues for teachers to grow and develop in the classroom. These opportunities need to be self-directed and cost neutral.

The reality is, our observations and interviews with teachers rated as strong PBL implementers show that they differ in terms of the individuals' increased tolerance for ambiguity, change, and risk. Their increased capacity for reflective practice is also a factor. In short, they can handle cognitive dissonance. When we prioritize investing in teacher growth, teachers rise to the occasion. And great things happen.

Challenges

Despite the strong reasons why it is so important to build the capacity of teachers, providing effective professional learning can be challenging. These challenges can vary based on education systems, resources, and local contexts, but here are some common challenges that we have seen in our work. These challenges remain consistent across all of the school districts working with us on this federally-funded, national project.

Time Constraints and Teacher Burnout

First and foremost, time is always a challenge. Even before the post-pandemic struggle to find substitute teachers, time was an issue. Teachers have demanding schedules with teaching, lesson planning, grading, and (my favorite part of many teacher contracts) *other duties as required*. Finding time for PL without disrupting classroom activities can be difficult. Additionally, intense workloads and stress make it difficult to engage in professional learning activities without distraction. Our team has seen this in our problem-based learning (PBL) professional learning. It is difficult to convince principals and teachers that the time is worth it. Even when teachers want to be in professional learning, there are constraints with competing priorities.

In one district, we were scheduled to do a two-day professional learning session. Day one was scheduled on a protected district PL day, meaning central office professional learning priorities took precedence. Day two was scheduled on a protected school PL day, meaning school building-level professional learning priorities took precedence. There were two teachers who came on the first day, the protected district level PL day, with the understanding they were being released from the protected school PL day to attend the second day of our session. That afternoon they received a message from their principal to return to their school for the morning of the second day. Even so, they came back in the afternoon on the second day after their school PL session ended.

This was extraordinary to us. The second day was a Friday before students arrived in the building on Monday. The teachers had chosen to come back just before meeting new students. They wanted to finish what they had started with us, despite the start of school looming and new students arriving. Not only that, it also showed the many different directions in which teachers are pulled. It is easy to see how, rather than having committed and sustainable days for PL, teachers are now MacGyvering as a response to makeshift schedules in order to support something as important as their growth. The decision about how to prioritize their time is taken out of their hands and they must nimbly triage to come to PL.

One-Size-Fits-All Approaches

Much like the students in our classrooms, teachers have diverse needs and levels of experience. Generic professional learning programs that do not cater to individual needs are ineffective and demotivating. Professional learning that focuses solely on theoretical concepts and isn't directly applicable to teachers' daily work and classroom needs may be seen as irrelevant and quickly forgotten (Hill & Papay, 2022). Professional learning needs to take into consideration the context of the district or school and the varying expertise of those in the room.

Too many sessions are set up as one-size-fits-all opportunities while the subject may only be valuable to a small set of teachers. For others, it's wasted time. These types of training sessions leave teachers without actionable strategies and lead to frustration.

This is so prevalent that many times, teachers walk into our professional learning with low to no expectations. Their body language often says it all at the beginning. A short time later, we see teachers with their laptops closed and phones set aside. This is because our design is significantly different from traditional PL. Our professional learning is heavily focused on the process. It sets the stage for the rest of the day by demonstrating that learning is socially constructed and, therefore, dependent on the contribution of multiple perspectives. During this initial impression, judgment is withheld about right or wrong answers. All questions and comments are accepted and examined.

Sustainability and Lack of Follow Up

Another challenge noted by Hill and Papay (2022) and echoed by many blogs and articles in *Education Week* is that one-off workshops or short-term programs are not likely to lead to lasting changes in teaching practice. As we have seen in our work with teachers across the country, continuous and sustained professional learning is required to see meaningful improvements. And because isolation in teaching can hinder the exchange of ideas and collaborative learning among teachers, PL should be followed by ongoing support and coaching to help teachers to implement new strategies effectively. As a result, follow-up support is built into our training opportunities.

There is only so much that can be absorbed in one sitting. Our process prioritizes sequencing content just in time. What do teachers need first to leave our sessions understanding and being able to teach PBL? We then follow up with sessions that build on the skills teachers need to be successful before they teach their first PBL unit, offer individual coaching, and provide additional sessions after they teach to reflect on their PBL experiences and refine their practice. It is a comprehensive approach that makes implementation more sustainable.

Change Overload

There is only so much change a person can take at a time. Given the tendency in education to chase one initiative after another, it is understandable to be wary of change. Some teachers may be resistant to adopting new teaching methods or technologies due to familiarity or comfort with traditional practice, fear of failure, lack of confidence, or doubt that the new initiative will be sustained. Adequate support from school administrators is crucial for the successful implementation of professional learning initiatives. Without their backing, initiatives will falter.

Paying attention to administrator support is especially important with a teaching practice like PBL, which disrupts a lot of commonly held ideas about what happens in the classroom, as we have already discussed. Problem-based learning is student-directed and requires a teacher to drastically change their practice. In a PBL unit, the teacher's role shifts to facilitator and metacognitive coach and there are new skillsets required to successfully take on this role. As a result, our training specifically builds confidence and efficacy around these required skills and helps teachers to see why this approach is so beneficial for students, thereby motivating them to invest the time needed to adapt to the change.

Despite the many challenges in designing and leading professional learning, our team is dedicated. By addressing the implementation of tailored solutions, we enhance the impact of the professional learning and, in turn, improve the quality of teaching and the quality of life of teachers. We have also seen the ExCEL Model improve learning experiences for students. After all, that is the end game: improving learning for students. This is why Anne, Kim, and I have worked so hard to address these challenges and focus on what works in our PBL professional learning.

The Path Forward

Making the ExCEL Model work did not happen all at once. It took strategic and intentional iterations of planning, piloting, and evaluating results. Our team focused on what worked by putting modeling at the heart of the problem-based professional learning experience. We embedded coaching and collaboration as integral to the learning process. As we will explain, we learned what needed to be refined and sharpened our focus. We will share what ongoing support looked like and the impact of the program. You will see summaries of the lesson plans for the problem-based professional learning program and we will describe how to get started with it. We will discuss where research is headed and what we have learned from working with districts across the nation.

References

America Succeeds. (2023). *No worker left behind.* https://americasucce
    eds.org/wp-content/uploads/2023/04/No-Worker-Left-Behind-
    America-Succeeds.pdf
Bland, L. C., Horak, A. K., & Xu, X. (2018). Cognitive apprenticeship
    reflection tool [Unpublished measure]. George Mason University.
Darling-Hammond, L., & Cook-Harvey, C. (2018). *Educating the whole
    child: Improving school climate to support student success.* Learning
    Policy Institute. https://doi.org/10.54300/145.655
Dweck, C. S. (2006). *Mindset: The new psychology of success.* Random House.
Gay, G. (2018). *Culturally responsive teaching: Theory, research, and prac-
    tice.* (3rd ed.). Teachers College Press.
Guskey, T. R. (1986). Staff development and the process of teacher
    change. *Educational Researcher, 15*(5), 5–12. https://doi.org/10.3102/
    0013189X015005005

Hill, H. C., & Papay, J. P. (2022). *Building better PL: How to strengthen teacher learning.* Research Partnership for Professional Learning. https://annenberg.brown.edu/sites/default/files/rppl-building-bet ter-pl.pdf

Jacob, A., & McGovern, K. (2015). *The mirage: Confronting the hard truth about our quest for teacher development.* TNTP. https://tntp. org/assets/documents/TNTP-Mirage_2015.pdf

Ladson-Billings, G. (2021). *Culturally relevant pedagogy: Asking a different question.* Teachers College Press.

Leu, E. (2005). The role of teachers, schools, and communities in quality education: A review of the literature. *Academy for Educational Development.* https://eric.ed.gov/?id=ED490174

Mandinach, E. B., & Gummer, E. S. (2016). What does it mean for teachers to be data literate: Laying out the skills, knowledge, and dispositions. *Teaching and Teacher Education, 60,* 366–376. https:// doi.org/10.1016/j.tate.2016.07.011

Olsen, B., & Wyss, M. C. (2022). *Teachers can change the world: Scaling quality teacher professional development.* https://www.brookings.edu/ articles/teachers-can-change-the-world-scaling-quality-teacher-professional-development/

Opfer, V. D., & Pedder, D. (2011). Conceptualizing teacher professional learning. *Review of Educational Research, 81*(3), 376–407. https:// doi.org/10.3102/0034654311413609

Rios, F., Trent, A., & Castaneda, L. V. (2010). Social perspective taking: Advancing empathy and advocating justice. *Equity and Excellence in Education, 36*(1), 5–14. https://doi.org/10.1080/106 65680303506

Schön, D. A. (1983). *The reflective practitioner: How professionals think in action.* Basic Books.

Chapter 6

Successfully Implementing PBL for Professional Learning

Shannon King

Focusing on What Works

From the work of Darling-Hammond et al. (2014), we know successful professional learning incorporates effective, research-based strategies, such as modeling, coaching, and collaboration, with social accountability. If you think back to the example of Anne's PBL professional learning that I shared earlier, these strategies may sound familiar. Our PBL professional learning is successful and effective because it draws on these research-based strategies to engage teachers and lay the groundwork for long-term implementation and fidelity.

     DOI: 10.4324/9781003452461-9

Modeling

When teachers embrace new approaches to their craft, they are taking on a lot. If we want to help teachers to be successful in risking trying something new or stepping out of their comfort zone, we need to create a safe space. We need to show what success looks like so they can visualize themselves implementing the idea, strategy, or approach. In short, we need to model it. An important first step in planning professional learning is getting clear about the strategies that are essential to your intended outcomes so you can incorporate a way to model these strategies. For our federally-funded project, this meant creating a professional learning experience that modeled a problem-based learning narrative and mirrored the strategies teachers would need to facilitate PBL in the classroom.

When it comes to modeling, adult learning theory plays a role. Adults learn differently from children. Modeling, when not respecting adult learning needs, can alienate the audience. I remember one uncomfortable experience when a professional learning facilitator taught us like we were students in an elementary language arts lesson. I was never sure if I should answer her questions as myself or as a third grader. It distracted me from understanding what she wanted us to see and more than that, it felt condescending. When we talk about modeling, we plan to model the experience in a way that is appropriate for adults. This means that you may use an instructional strategy with a relevant topic for teachers. In this way, they can see the strategy in action while engaging with a topic that matters for them. In our professional learning, this was the thrust behind changing the focus from modeling a student unit to modeling a problem of professional practice with which they could identify or may have even recently come across in their PLC sessions.

Modeling was one of the most compelling aspects of Anne's PBL professional learning. The educators were actively engaged in a PBL experience, which had the intention of inviting the participants to:

◈   Feel what is like to have more questions than answers;

◈   See how facilitators use metacognitive coaching to push thinking;

◈   Experience the autonomy of directing their learning; and

◈   Engage as stakeholders working to define and address a problem.

Getting the approach to modeling right is so important that we continue to refine our approach. The first professional learning session for teachers used an existing PBL unit focused on the history of the Bubonic Plague. While that was interesting and worked well, subsequent revisions strengthened the PL by creating a PBL for teachers using a problem of professional practice. In this problem, teachers are put in a stakeholder role as team of educators implementing PBL. Their principal asks the team to help him to address a challenge raised by another educator. This keeps the focus on modeling the intended outcomes while taking into consideration the needs of adult learners. It makes it feel age appropriate and less staged. The problem of professional practice sustains participation and inspires genuine interaction.

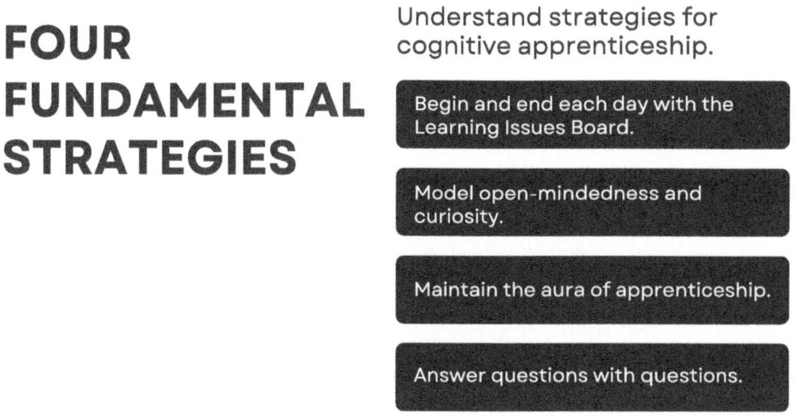

FOUR FUNDAMENTAL STRATEGIES

Understand strategies for cognitive apprenticeship.

Begin and end each day with the Learning Issues Board.

Model open-mindedness and curiosity.

Maintain the aura of apprenticeship.

Answer questions with questions.

Figure 6.1 Four strategies for creating equity.

Project ExCEL-Ignite | Letterpress Communications

One of the reasons for this may be because the scenario is relevant and something teachers may realistically have to address.

Collaboration

We know information is best retained when we can process it with others. That is why collaboration is a powerful tool for teacher learning. The Professional Learning Community (PLC) work of DuFour et al. (2016) shows that building and training collaborative teams as part of teachers' practice is effective because it creates a structured space for teachers to talk about the ideas they learn. It provides a process and the opportunity for teachers to challenge ideas, build on each other's understanding, and think about how those ideas may work in their current context. Collaboration embodies the proverb, "If you want to go fast, go alone. If you want to go far, go together."

We have seen collaboration work as an important part of professional learning settings. It provides teachers with opportunities to think out loud about the ideas being shared. It gives them an avenue to test ideas and challenge thinking. It makes space for teachers to unpack a new concept or strategy. It also sends the message that they are not alone. Teachers do not have to try this strategy out by themselves. They have teammates that are also trying it out, so there are others around to support them.

Accessibility is another reason collaboration has an impact on teachers' professional learning. Many schools have built-in time for teacher collaboration. This is a convenient opportunity to embed learning into everyday practice. It provides an ongoing opening to return to ideas and reinforce them. It gives teachers a chance to try things out and then come back and reflect together. It avoids the one and done approach that teachers are so used to when it comes to professional learning. We know this doesn't work (Jacob & McGovern, 2015; Opfer & Pedder, 2011). And yet, we still do it. I know, I'm shaking my head too. With the ExCEL Model, we leverage the existing structures of PLCs within schools to capitalize on collaboration as a means for reflection and setting goals for instruction. This happens when teachers use the Cognitive Apprenticeship Rubric with videos of their own instruction to analyze their practice and evaluate areas for growth.

Social Accountability

Accountability often feels punitive. It is usually discussed when something is going wrong. On the other hand, it can be productive. Social accountability can provide a sense of belonging to a collaborative team to which you feel a sense of responsibility. One thing that makes the social accountability aspect of the professional learning within the ExCEL Model especially powerful is that it is a process teachers go through together. Teachers start with professional learning, they implement PBL units, and they are coached throughout the process. They record themselves teaching and get many opportunities to talk about how implementation is going. It is a continuous improvement process. It is not a one and done notion.

There are individual moments of support in which teachers engage in coaching conversations. There are times when they come together and share how things went. When teachers share, they report what they noticed about students' reactions to moments in the unit, things that worked, and things that did not work especially well. They learn from each other's mistakes, celebrate each other's triumphs, and in general, bring a sense of ownership of the learning to the whole group. We have seen time and time again that collaboration is a powerful tool for professional learning. We have also seen that collaboration is most effective when a trained coach is there to support it.

Our process is a cycle that teachers spiral through. As they advance, the professional learning is customized to the learning needs they have, based on the personalized goals they set. The common denominator is that this is always done together. Although teachers are at their school sites and we are at the university, sometimes with hundreds of miles between us, we do not leave them to hang on their own at any point. We are partners; both with our teachers and school districts. It is a collaborative approach that provides plenty of social accountability.

Coaching

Coaching is an effective tool for improving teachers' practice (Hill & Papay, 2022). Incorporating coaching into professional learning provides an opportunity for ongoing support and adds a layer of accountability to professional learning. When teachers attend a professional learning session accompanied by follow-up coaching, they have the opportunity to try ideas out with support. In this paradigm, teachers are more inclined to try PBL because someone will be there and that person is there to help them. While coaching can be helpful for reflection and processing on the teacher's part, it also helps those facilitating the PL to really see how the learning from the session is implemented. It gives us a chance to look at how implementation is going and make refinements to future professional learning sessions, if necessary.

For the purposes of PBL curriculum implementation, this coaching is metacognitive coaching and so, it is also modeling. The coaching that supports metacognitive reflection for teachers in our work look like this. After the introductory PL session, teachers go back to their school and prepare for unit implementation. They select the unit, read it, and prepare materials for their students. Just before the unit, a member of the project team reaches out to check in and schedule a meeting. This meeting is to review any questions or concerns. Teachers ask several questions related to staying in the stakeholder role. They are concerned about stepping out of the role because they know more than the students do from reading and planning the unit. The coach captures data and then, in conversation, explains the importance of the stakeholder role and models some strategies for staying in it. This provides a starting point for teachers to move forward and creates a plan for getting back in to the stakeholder role if they find themselves slipping out of it. This initial conversation also sets the stage for further reflection after the unit is finished. This initial concern of staying in the stakeholder role has now also created an area of focus.

Coaching is personalized. Even in the same school and on the same grade level, every teacher has different needs. When teaching PBL for the first time, different teachers are apprehensive about different things. One teacher was worried about providing adequate scaffolding for the large number of multilingual learners in her class. As she prepared to teach her first PBL unit, she reached out to the project team. After learning more about her individual classes, one of our research assistants reviewed the readings in the unit and found several alternates that might be better for her students. Additionally, a coaching session was set up to specifically discuss grouping for the PBL unit as providing tasks and roles and focusing on student assets would be helpful in making her PBL facilitation successful. After coaching, the teacher felt more comfortable with PBL. She told us later during a debrief session that the conversation about grouping was helpful and she wanted to expand these ideas more when she implemented PBL the next year.

In the ExCEL Model, coaching is provided by facilitators both during sessions and in the form of coaching conversations that invite teachers and future trainers to reflect on their practice. It is also provided through video analysis, where teachers record themselves and then watch the videos with a coach to think through what they like about what they're seeing, what worked, and things that they would like to strive to improve moving forward.

These examples we have shared show how our ExCEL Model focuses on what works. And in order for professional learning to be effective, they show that we have:

1) Made sure we are teaching teachers in the way we want them to teach;

2) Provided opportunities for teachers to collaborate and make sense of their learning with others; and

3) Provided coaching support that allows teachers to reflect and integrate their learning in ways that are differentiated for them.

We cannot afford not to spend time on effective, intentional teacher professional learning. Anne, Kim, Dana, and I all believe this profoundly. We have seen it. We saw it as participants and now see it as the people who support teachers across the country as they tackle the learning trajectory of taking on the ExCEL Model.

There is so much good that can be done when we provide exemplary professional learning for teachers. In the following section, Anne will share an overview of the resources and materials that were created with these big ideas in mind. Remember that the professional learning program is extensive and ongoing. What you will see described in the next chapter is merely a snapshot. These materials were designed for you to be implemented and integrated into the things you are already doing. While you can pick up this book and implement these things on your own, to benefit from the full depth of our professional learning, I hope that you will choose to invite support from others on your journey to implement the ExCEL Model.

References

Darling-Hammond, L., Hyler, M. E., Gardner, M., & Espinoza, D. (2014). *Effective teacher professional development.* Learning Policy Institute. https://doi.org/10.54300/122.311

DuFour, R., DuFour, R., Eaker, R., Many, T., & Mattos, M. (2016). *Learning by doing: A handbook for professional learning communities at work.* (3rd ed.). Solution Tree.

Hill, H. C., & Papay, J. P. (2022). *Building better PL: How to strengthen teacher learning.* Research Partnership for Professional Learning. https://annenberg.brown.edu/sites/default/files/rppl-building-bet ter-pl.pdf

Jacob, A., & McGovern, K. (2015). *The mirage: Confronting the hard truth about our quest for teacher development.* TNTP. https://tntp. org/assets/documents/TNTP-Mirage_2015.pdf

Opfer, V. D., & Pedder, D. (2011). Conceptualizing teacher professional learning. *Review of Educational Research, 81*(3), 376–407. https:// doi.org/10.3102/0034654311413609

Chapter 7

The ExCEL Model Professional Learning Program

Anne Horak

It Started Like This

To share an overview of our resources and materials, I first need to pick back up again from where I left off in the introduction. From the vantage point of central office and with the mission my office had been tasked with, I had a vehicle to implement strategies and activities of consequence. I also had committed colleagues, like Shannon, with whom to collaborate. After landing on problem-based learning (PBL) curriculum as an effective instructional intervention, professional learning for teachers was the next logical step. Our district was resource rich and teachers were routinely provided with professional opportunities. In my first year in the district, I participated in more required professional learning days than I had in all previous years combined before I was hired in the district.

Our early sessions in the district included an abbreviated demonstration of a PBL curriculum unit. As Shannon mentioned, this was novel and engaging. For this reason, it was effective. Yet, the

95   DOI: 10.4324/9781003452461-10

Figure 7.1 The ExCEL Model.

Project ExCEL-Ignite | Letterpress Communications

engagement was not persuasive enough to convince teachers to make changes to their instructional practice. For this reason, it was not effective. From this experience, I learned a lot. Globally, change of any scale requires a model that is flexible enough to work in the real context of schools. Teachers would tell me they liked the PBL but did not know how to fit it into their pacing guide. Locally, competing priorities are real. Having been in the classroom for nearly a decade myself, I know exactly how much teachers care about their students and their instructional practice. Individually, teachers need to be met where they are. Understanding this in particular required me to be enlightened by the teachers I was trying so hard to enlighten. I needed first to learn what their needs were and second to align my objectives to those needs rather than the other way around.

Talk to any first-year teacher. Or any teacher, for that matter. Not a single one would say they went into teaching to make the lives of students worse. It took a good deal of intellectual humility to understand that if I wanted to support changes to instructional practice, I needed to understand barriers to those changes from the teachers' perspective. Later, our research confirmed these preliminary understandings and we found that scale, competing priorities, and teacher turnover were the three most significant threats to sustaining the ExCEL Model.

Our early professional learning sessions on PBL for our first Javits funding, Project ExCEL (Shaklee & Horak, 2014), and later our second Javits funding, Project ExCEL-Ignite (Horak & Shaklee, 2019), were based on what we had done in the first district. The sessions were two days in length. The sessions began by inviting teachers to participate in a demonstration of a student unit. This then continued, with the facilitator in the role of classroom teacher and our teachers in the role of students, throughout the first phase of problem-based learning, i.e., the initial Problem Engagement phase. Following the demonstration, the session continued with traditional teacher-directed segments on metacognitive coaching, gifted and diverse learners, identification policies, and underrepresented populations in gifted classes.

It Did Not Work, Entirely

Our framework provided teachers with an opportunity to feel the absorbing nature of an ill-structured problem. It allowed teachers to directly experience the compelling nature of leveraging curiosity as a motivation to learn. Unfortunately, it also primarily framed PBL as a novelty and distinct from the standard scope and sequence of teaching. We needed teachers to walk away understanding that the instructional skills needed for PBL transfer across teaching contexts and that PBL is a vehicle for the delivery of standards. The solution was clear. We needed to keep teachers in the problem narrative for the entire duration of the professional learning.

We quickly, and slightly painfully, learned that keeping the teachers in the role of students throughout the problem narrative after Problem Engagement was patronizing. Earlier, Shannon detailed the confusion she felt when she attended a professional learning session where the instructor treated her like a third grader. At times, we have had teachers reenact challenging student behaviors. This marginalized our objective of modeling by effectively shutting down thinking rather than opening it up. Maybe, just maybe, those teachers were illustrating to us the exact condescension of modeling that we had unintentionally illustrated for them by keeping them in the student role. Modeling by situating teachers as students had limits. It was not that modeling itself was inappropriate. It was the role of the participant that drove the effectiveness.

Again, the solution was clear. The problem-based learning experience needed to be a problem in which teachers were in the stakeholder role of teachers tasked with solving a problem of professional practice. We were excited and stumped. What problem of professional practice had the depth and complexity to effectively explore problem-based learning? We thought about this for a long time.

We proposed one idea, and then another. None held together under the weight of the many objectives we had and was in alignment with the evidence-based practice for professional learning. Until it occurred to me. I wish I could remember what exactly triggered the thought. The idea felt like a flash flood in my brain. The problem was the problem. Underrepresentation. Diverse gifted learners. Challenging curriculum. Teacher professional learning. A grant. The problem was the problem.

Remember Dana, my colleague and our curriculum development consultant? I called her. "The problem is the problem! The problem is the problem! Why are looking for a problem when we were already working on a problem?" I asked her. "Now, we have a different problem," she told me. "Now, we have to write it."

As discussed earlier, the model of our problem-based learning curriculum is grounded and begins with the Problem Engagement phase. This is when learners are immersed in the problem and learn that there is some urgency to it. So, to begin, we wrote the Problem Engagement memo. In the Problem Engagement, we situated teachers participating in the professional learning in the stakeholder role of members of the English language arts department at Sunnyside Middle School. As members of the English language arts department at Sunnyside Middle School, they receive a complaint from their feeder high school about the way they are identifying students for gifted classes. They have a few days to gather information to present to the high school. We piloted it once. We learned it had potential. The problem was compelling and relevant. But it needed more testing and we were running out of time. The performance period of our Javits grant was ending in nine months.

We applied for and received a second round of funding. The focus was on scaling up and implementation at a distance from the university. Just as we were preparing for the professional learning, COVID-19 shut down the world and our university mandated that we suspend all travel and school-based research activities. We threw ourselves into preparing to hit the ground running when given the all clear to resume travel and school-based work. This included writing the professional learning problem-based curriculum in full. We already had the first version of the Problem Engagement memo. We wrote the accompanying lesson for the Problem Engagement phase. Then, we mapped out the rest of the problem narrative and wrote the lessons and memos for the Inquiry and Investigation, Problem Definition, Problem Resolution, and Problem Debrief phases. As a result, we had a complete professional learning problem-based curriculum unit available in a format that could be replicated with a high degree of fidelity. This was crucial for consistency and quality. The solidity of it being printed, hole punched, and neatly tucked into a 2-inch binder with dividers, quite frankly, made what we had done before look slipshod. Yet, it still needed more testing.

After two rounds of implementation, we had gathered enough evidence to suggest the new format that resolved the initial concerns. After participating in the problem-based segment of the professional learning, teachers reported that they understood what PBL is and felt prepared to teach it. They reported feeling engaged during the professional learning and that they acquired important content.

Yet, in the post-COVID world, substitute teachers were scarce. Regardless of how engaging and meaningful the session, two days was a luxury that was no longer possible. Our districts were pushing us to offer the session in one day or online. Our professional learning needed to evolve again.

What We Did

Our problem-based professional learning needed to evolve. It needed to be compacted. It needed to be sustainable. Considering this, an online option was appealing. We decided to pursue it. Some elements of PBL did not translate easily to an online format. During PBL, the teacher manages the Learning Issues Board by writing down facts that the group learns, recording any questions the group has, and capturing hunches about what is happening. One important function of the teacher is to make connections between hunches, questions, and facts. As in, if this is our hunch, what question do we need to answer in order to learn a fact that would confirm this information. The teacher uses metacognitive coaching to drive students to identify the gaps in their knowledge so they can formulate questions. This is all done in a continuous, collaborative loop. Hunch, question, fact. Hunch, question, fact. The group collaboration aspect is important. The teacher responds to questions with questions, which may prompt another student's thinking, who then contributes with a clarification and another question. The teacher models open-mindedness and curiosity and pushes for explanations and depth of understanding. While self-directed research was possible to translate to an online format, a teacher's expertise and craft of instructional practice plays such a critical role in driving students to high-quality reasoning that could not be replicated entirely online.

And there was still the issue of delivering the professional learning in one day.

We were preoccupied by considering how to deliver the content-heavy PBL professional learning curriculum in one day while maintaining the integrity of the experience and the content acquisition needed to prepare teachers to teach PBL. In other words, what could we leave out? To answer this question, we turned mainly to the Learning Issues Board (LIB). This board, as described in the chapter on educational change, reflects a group's progress through the problem. Both facts and questions are recorded on it. During professional learning, teachers prioritize the questions on the Learning Issues Board. An examination of this revealed patterns in how teachers had prioritized the content and skills. In other words, we saw the questions teachers were asking unfolded in a sequence that repeated itself over time. Across LIBs from different sessions, we saw that many questions were asked about certain topics and few questions were asked about others. We recorded and examined how the time spent on each topic in each session varied. This data helped to determine the content and skills that were priorities for teachers and, therefore, what content and skills we could compact.

We then examined these compacted lessons for alignment to the literature. We made sure that we were teaching teachers in the way we wanted them to teach by carrying out problem-based professional learning for every learning objective. We built in opportunities for teachers to collaborate and make sense of their learning with others throughout the session. We made sure that the coaching support that allowed them to reflect and integrate their learning in ways that were differentiated for them spiraled consistently throughout the experience.

What It Looks Like Now

Every project has a starting point, and ours began with understanding the ExCEL Model problem-based professional learning program. Problem-based learning is characterized by five phases, beginning with Problem Engagement, moving into Inquiry and Investigation, Problem Definition, and Problem Resolution, and ending with Problem Debrief. The lesson summaries presented in the following pages align to those phases and provide a conceptual over-view of the problem-based learning curriculum for the professional learning program that, when implemented with fidelity, ultimately results in positive outcomes.

To set the stage, our professional learning begins with a concept development exercise focused on the topic of barriers. Following that, the session transitions into the Problem Engagement phase, during which teachers are introduced to their stakeholder role as members of the English language arts department at a middle school implementing the ExCEL Model. The ill-structured problem is designed so that the constraint they are facing is a complaint from the feeder high school. This launches them into the Inquiry and Investigation phase, during which they research problem-based learning curriculum and instruc-tion, identification and underrepresentation, giftedness and diverse learners, and data and outcomes. This information is synthesized during the Problem Definition phase in order to clarify the task and plan a response. Following this, teachers organize their research to form problem resolutions. Finally, in the Problem Debrief phase, the process is unveiled to give participants time to analyze and evaluate the method.

Progressive Support

Exploratory support for the professional learning program, including summaries of the strategies and activities that take place during each phase of the problem-based professional learning, are included in this book. You will be introduced to the accompanying resources and materials and provided with examples of facilitator tips that support the effective implementation of the problem-based professional learning program. These summaries are an abbreviated version of our lessons and are intended to familiarize you with what makes this program exciting.

There is more. Elevated support includes access to the extended forms of the professional learning lessons. The professional learning program was designed alongside the implementation of problem-based learning curriculum in middle school classrooms. The curriculum is aligned to standards for students in P-12. While most of our examples come from our experience in middle school, the lessons learned here still apply to secondary and elementary contexts.

For those of you who want to go further, there is even more. Multidimensional, concentrated support includes guided practice, as well as expert coaching and feedback. If you find the professional learning program appealing, we strongly encourage you to check out the P-12-aligned problem-based learning curriculum and seek experts to work with who can provide this coaching and feedback for you and your team.

Like effective classroom instruction, the lessons we use that are presented here are meant to be flexible enough to be delivered in a variety of formats. We have tested delivering the program in one day of in-person sessions, during which each segment or core topic took somewhere between 30–90 minutes, depending on the group. We have delivered it online and in a hybrid format. We have had teacher leaders deliver it to grade-level teams during PLC meetings. Which way to deliver it depends on what makes the most sense for your context.

Problem-based learning is intentionally designed to be self-directed. The lessons are presented in the order that our experience has shown aligns with how teachers prioritize their learning issues. Therefore, this is typically how the research then unfolds. However, the sessions are meant to be flexible and implemented in any order based on how teachers prioritize their research issues. It is helpful to keep in mind that each implementation may go in a different order. Each segment of the professional learning program provides opportunities for teachers to reflect. Opportunities for the professional learning facilitator to pre-assess and post-assess are embedded into the problem-based learning process along the way.

LESSON: CONCEPT DEVELOPMENT

Lesson Length
45 Minutes

Goal: Explore high-level instructional strategy.
Key Question: What do we know about barriers?

Participants engage in a Taba's Model exercise centered on the topic of "Barriers." Concept development is a cornerstone of Problem-based learning curriculum. This sets the stage for learning by engaging participants in the type of critical, creative, and problem-solving skills that are key for understanding the problem they will encounter in the Problem Engagement.

Lesson Handouts

- 5-Steps Template and Directions
- Universal Concepts and Generalizations

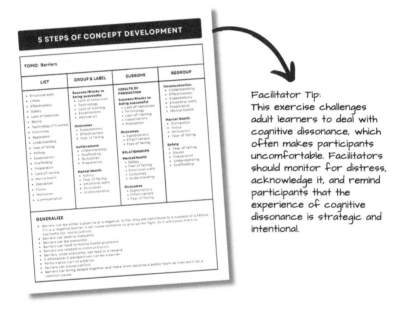

Facilitator Tip:
This exercise challenges adult learners to deal with cognitive dissonance, which often makes participants uncomfortable. Facilitators should monitor for distress, acknowledge it, and remind participants that the experience of cognitive dissonance is strategic and intentional.

Figure 7.2 Getting started: concept development.

Project ExCEL-Ignite | Letterpress Communications

LESSON: PROBLEM ENGAGEMENT

Lesson Length
45 Minutes

Goal: Develop and prioritize issues.
Key Question: What is our role in this problem?

Participants are introduced to their stakeholder roles as members of the Project ExCEL Lead Team at Sunnyside MS. They receive a voicemail from their principal, Mr. Dearson. He explains that the English department from Harbor Dale High School has concerns the newly identified gifted students from Sunnyside MS will be set up to fail in high school. The Harbor Dale teachers threaten to go to the School Board with their concerns. In an effort to deescalate the situation, the Sunnyside MS team has an opportunity to explain the benefits of the new identification process to the Harbor Dale English department teachers.

Lesson Handouts
- Voicemail Transcription from Terrance to ExCEL Lead Team
- Kicker #1 Harbor Dale High School Concerns

Facilitator Tip:
First, drive participants to understand their stakeholder role. Some groups settle into it more smoothly than others. Drive them toward understanding the problem, learning issues, task, and deadline. However, avoid feeding them information. There will be multiple opportunities for all of this to emerge.

Figure 7.3 Problem Engagement.
Project ExCEL-Ignite | Letterpress Communications

LESSON: INQUIRY & INVESTIGATION PROBLEM-BASED LEARNING

Lesson Length
50 Minutes

Goal: Research questions and apply new learnings.
Key Question: What is problem-based learning?

Participants conduct research on problem-based learning (PBL), why it is relevant in modern classrooms, the associated educational outcomes, and the barriers to implementation. Participants are given time to review PBL curriculum and how it aligns with national, state, and local standards.

Lesson Handouts

- Memo #1 - Resource Teacher
- Elements of PBL and Inquiry & Investigation Handout
- ESSA Support for ExCEL
- Inquiry & Investigation Universal Reflective Moment

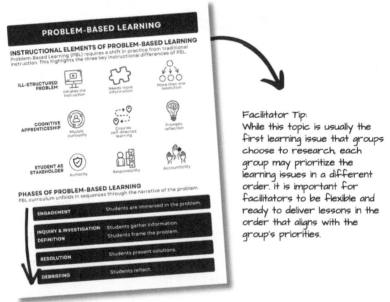

Facilitator Tip:
While this topic is usually the first learning issue that groups choose to research, each group may prioritize the learning issues in a different order. It is important for facilitators to be flexible and ready to deliver lessons in the order that aligns with the group's priorities.

Figure 7.4 Inquiry and Investigation: understanding problem-based learning.

Project ExCEL-Ignite | Letterpress Communications

LESSON: INQUIRY & INVESTIGATION IDENTIFICATION AND DIVERSE LEARNERS

Lesson Length
45 Minutes

Goal: Research and apply new information.
Key Question: Who are gifted and diverse learners? How do we identify them?

Participants research their prioritized learning issues from the previous lesson and conduct targeted research on traditional identification methods and underrepresentation; giftedness; and culturally, linguistically, and economically diverse learners.

Lesson Handouts

- Memo #3 Email from Giftedness and Diverse Learners Expert
- Attributes in Action
- Inquiry and Investigation Universal Reflective Moment

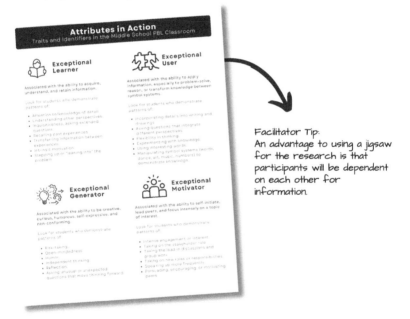

Figure 7.5 Inquiry and Investigation: identification of diverse learners.
Project ExCEL-Ignite | Letterpress Communications

LESSON: INQUIRY & INVESTIGATION METACOGNITIVE COACHING

Lesson Length **55** Minutes

Goal: Research problem and apply new information.
Key Question: What is metacognitive coaching?

Participants research their prioritized learning issues from the previous lesson and conduct targeted research on metacognitive coaching. They learn that metacognitive coaching often means implementing new instructional skills.

Lesson Handouts
- Kicker #2 Email from Concerned Parent
- Cognitive Apprenticeship Rubric and Guide for Use
- Inquiry and Investigation Universal Reflective Moment

Facilitator Tip:
As the facilitator, you are modeling metacognitive coaching at all times. It is important to support participants' understanding that teaching characterized by metacognitive coaching is a skill that can be measured on a continuum. Growth towards expertise is the goal.

Figure 7.6 Inquiry and Investigation: modeling metacognitive coaching.
Project ExCEL-Ignite | Letterpress Communications

LESSON: INQUIRY & INVESTIGATION DATA AND EVIDENCE

Lesson Length
45 Minutes

Goal: Research and apply new information.
Key Question: What are the outcomes of implementing the ExCEL Model for participants and students?

Participants research their prioritized learning issues from the previous lesson and conduct targeted research on the educational outcomes of using the ExCEL Model. Participants discuss the impact on students' achievement and engagement, discover the impact on equity for gifted identification, and learn how participants' beliefs about instruction and giftedness are influenced by ExCEL Model implementation.

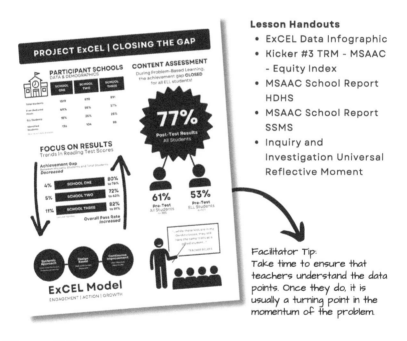

Lesson Handouts
- ExCEL Data Infographic
- Kicker #3 TRM - MSAAC - Equity Index
- MSAAC School Report HDHS
- MSAAC School Report SSMS
- Inquiry and Investigation Universal Reflective Moment

Facilitator Tip:
Take time to ensure that teachers understand the data points. Once they do, it is usually a turning point in the momentum of the problem.

Figure 7.7 Inquiry and Investigation: using data and evidence.
Project ExCEL-Ignite | Letterpress Communications

LESSON: PROBLEM DEFINITION

Lesson Length
20 Minutes

Goal: Clearly define the problem.
Key Question: What is the problem?
                        What are the constraints?

Participants use everything that they have learned about problem-based learning is, to create a clear problem definition. Once participants have defined the problem, they work together to come to a consensus about how to craft talking points for Mr. Dearson to take to the meeting.

Lesson Handouts
- Fishbone Diagram Template
- Problem Definition Template

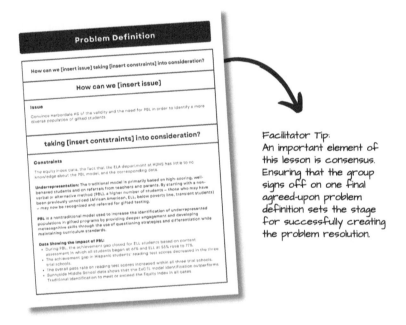

Facilitator Tip:
An important element of this lesson is consensus. Ensuring that the group signs off on one final agreed-upon problem definition sets the stage for successfully creating the problem resolution.

Figure 7.8 Problem Definition.

Project ExCEL-Ignite | Letterpress Communications

LESSON: PROBLEM RESOLUTION

Lesson Length
20 Minutes

Goal: Clearly articulate the problem.
Key Question: How do we clearly articulate the problem?

Participants prioritize and divide the workload so that each group takes a global topic and works together to develop 1-3 talking points.

Lesson Handouts
- Memo #5 - Time Constraint Option 1 Criteria or Option 2 Judgement
- HDHS ELA DEPT Meeting Agenda
- Reflective Moment – Problem Resolution

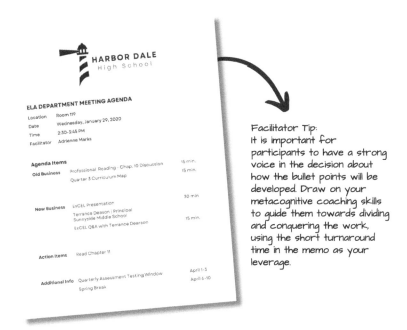

Figure 7.9 Problem Resolution.
Project ExCEL-Ignite | Letterpress Communications

LESSON: PROBLEM DEBRIEFING

Lesson Length
20 Minutes

Goal: Summarize learning and discuss next steps.
Key Question: What are your key takeaways?

This lesson takes place after the narrative arc of the problem has ended. The stages of Problem-Based Learning are reviewed and aligned to the sessions the participants experienced. Participants summarize their takeaways from the learning, process remaining questions and concerns, and discuss next steps.

Lesson Handouts

- Unit Summaries ExCEL-Ignite Handout
- State and District PBL Curriculum Unit Alignments

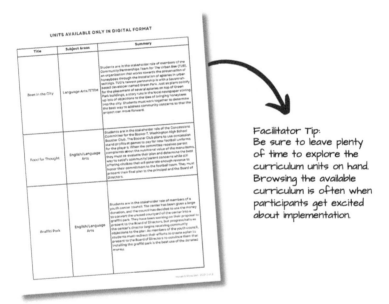

Facilitator Tip:
Be sure to leave plenty of time to explore the curriculum units on hand. Browsing the available curriculum is often when participants get excited about implementation.

Figure 7.10 Problem Debrief.
Project ExCEL-Ignite | Letterpress Communications

It is also important to keep in mind that what you have here is an overview of the curriculum that is embedded within a comprehensive model, which includes professional learning, curriculum development, and continuous improvement. It also includes ongoing professional learning that spirals through these key concepts repeatedly and with increasing depth.

Outcomes and Impacts

Our work has always been focused on problem-based learning. But even though most of this book has been dedicated to our professional learning program, we have seen some other amazing program outcomes that are worth mentioning. First, the rigorous and high-level problem-based learning curriculum we developed and made available to teachers has been requested in over 35 US states and several countries around the world. Our curriculum is not only requested by those who work with Gifted and Talented programs but also those who work with other advanced courses and magnet programs, as well as core content teachers. Eight of our PBL units have also received curriculum awards from the National Association of Gifted Children.

Although our federally-funded project started with using PBL as a universal screening method for potential in English language arts classes, we have found that it can be taught successfully in other courses that all students take (and still be used as a universal screening method). Over the course of two rounds of funding, we have provided professional learning and coaching support to science and social studies teachers, in addition to those whose primary designation is working with multilingual learners and supporting students with special educational needs. Our team has also been approached by teachers who would like to teach PBL in elective courses, such as specialized STEM courses and AVID (Advancement Via Individual Determination).

Teachers see the value of using PBL to help gifted and advanced students to build global citizenship, sustainability, and global competence skills. As these topics are not taught as standalone subjects in any US state, PBL (with its transdisciplinary connections) can be used to develop leadership, collaboration, and advocacy skills in students while also developing content, critical thinking, and problem-solving skills.

Another interesting outcome we have seen over time is the development of researchers in the area of problem-based learning. While working on this large research project, we have employed and mentored 29 doctoral and undergraduate research assistants. These students not only assist with our work with schools but are also introduced to issues concerning equity and social justice in gifted education. Our work, which is centered on the real-world conditions of schools, provides a training ground for students who want to build skills concerning teaching pedagogies, gifted education, underrepresentation and equity, and the complexities of school environments.

Finally, our most exciting outcome is probably related to our professional learning curriculum and this book. Our effort may be the first of its kind to provide professional learning for PBL with a direct connection to the identification of gifted learners. We specifically developed this program using our knowledge of the social justice and equity issues in gifted education, but we also understand the complexities of gifted education in the US. This book provides a starting point for those who are working on their own or do not have the resources of a large school district. It is a bridge for those who want to know where to begin.

Where the Research is Heading

When we started this work, the focus was on can PBL do it? Can PBL increase achievement and engagement while being used as a universal screening method with a dynamic performance assessment to increase the identification of culturally, linguistically, and economically diverse students for advanced and gifted classes? The answer was yes, but not alone. The singular act of implementing PBL in the classroom is insufficient for achieving the goal of finding underrepresented students. Professional learning and continuous improvement are critical elements that constitute a comprehensive model.

As our program has developed, the questions have shifted. Following where the research is leading, we now wonder: what makes professional learning effective? Along with the question of can we measure teachers' growth as a result? This is where we are going. We have the tools to do that. The Cognitive Apprenticeship Rubric (CAR) is a measure we developed and validated to measure teacher growth within a skillset that is specific to problem-based learning. To teach PBL successfully, it is critical for teachers to apply a specific skillset that develops the key elements of PBL, including student discovery within problem-solving and scaffolding students' successful critical, creative, and metacognitive thinking skills. Not only that, but the Cognitive Apprenticeship Rubric has applications for research that tie student outcomes to teacher professional learning.

Conclusion

Developing effective professional learning for educators is a challenge. And yet, it is essential that we get it right, so we can support teachers by engaging them as learners. So teachers can build capacity and opportunities to grow within the context of their classroom. So we have the will and skill to innovate our practice to stay up to date on best practice. So we can best prepare our students for their futures.

Our team has developed, reflected on, and refined various versions of our problem-based professional learning program, all in the pursuit of making the lives of teachers and students better. That is the first and last reason why we have worked tirelessly to provide the best and most effective evidence-based professional learning experience possible.

Now that we have some evidence that what we are doing is working, the next step is to spread, scale, and sustain. The threats to sustainability are many. Yet, teacher turnover, competing priorities, and scale create the most ambiguity about the capacity to implement the program. We have encountered these challenges in every state, every district, and every school. It is a misconception to think that these threats to sustainability need to be removed in order for the program to be successful. Categorically, teacher turnover will always be a challenge.

Rather, if ambiguity can be tolerated until a plan is formed, solutions that bring stability can be found. Solutions that are design-based and contextual. This is the importance of our model being flexible and adaptable. What are those contextual solutions? As we bring this story to a close, we will share some of the ways in which we have adapted the model to address sustainability.

References

Horak, A., & Shaklee, B. (2019). *Project E-Ignite*. U.S. Department of Education, Javits Gifted and Talented Students Education Grant Program.

Shaklee, B., & Horak, A. (2014). *Project ExCEL*. U.S. Department of Education, Institute of Educational Sciences, Javits Gifted and Talented Students Education Grant Program.

Closing

Anne Horak

In the preface, we told you that through this book, we would provide you with an understanding of problem-based learning, the tools and information needed to support teachers in professional growth, a road map for implementing and sustaining an evidence-based continuous improvement program model, and evidence broadening the literature base that supports increasing equity and access. We have shared how the ExCEL Model came to be. We have explained how the problem-based learning curriculum is the cornerstone for this model and the foundation on which all the outcomes for change are built. We have provided the context for change given considerations related to equity and access in gifted education. We have discussed how we designed the professional learning program specifically to align to our PBL curriculum and reflect best practice for adult learners. In the closing, we will share how to know you are applying the ExCEL Model in practice, our most significant takeaways and reflections, and the direction we see our work heading.

Applying the ExCEL Model in Practice

The ExCEL Model is a system that has been proven to be effective by a continuous line of federally-funded research supported by the US

    DOI: 10.4324/9781003452461-11

Figure 8.1 The ExCEL Model.

Project ExCEL-Ignite | Letterpress Communications

Department of Education Jacob K. Javits Program. Project ExCEL (Shaklee & Horak, 2014), our first proposal for research, brought together several research strands to form a practical application that could be applied in schools. From that practical application, the parts that worked were woven into a system called the ExCEL Model. Project ExCEL-Ignite (Horak & Shaklee, 2019), our second proposal for research, continued the implementation of the ExCEL Model system to understand the core elements necessary to carry out the model successfully in different school contexts.

ExCEL is an acronym for Experiences Cultivating Exceptional Learning. It reflects a focus on process and a growth mindset. The ExCEL Model engages school systems on many levels to take action leading to growth, specifically for teachers and students but also programmatically. The ExCEL Model encompasses all six of the National Association of Gifted Children gifted programming standards (National Association for Gifted Children, 2019), including learning and development, assessment, curriculum planning and instruction, learning environments, programing, and professional learning. It is grounded by the principles of design-based research (Brown, 1992). It was developed in the context of a gifted program facing real-world problems. It is a continuous improvement approach. Data are collected in rapid cycles and implementation is adjusted accordingly as changes and improvements are made.

There is the educational change strand, the curriculum and identification strand, and the professional learning strand. There is a flow.

It begins with professional learning and the implementation of PBL curriculum, moves to the identification of students, and continues to the measurement of results. The flow picks back up with professional learning and the cycle starts again. To know you are following the model means that you are intentionally attending to all the strands in this flow. If you are doing any of these individually, it is good for you and for your students, but it is not the model. If you are implementing these in isolation, then it is not the model. If you are implementing these in combination as a structure with a team as a support system, you are implementing a powerful model of school change and improvement that leads to equity.

The ExCEL Model Coming-of-Age Story

This story has been something of a professional coming-of-age story as much as it has been anything else. The journey began with a single adventurer. Likeminded companions joined the expedition along the way. There were setbacks. Specific setbacks that threatened sustainability, with competing priorities, turnover, and scale being the threats that made the project the most vulnerable. The group rose to the occasion to directly confront these threats to sustainability. We shifted our thinking to see them as informative and in doing so, gained insight, perspective, and stability.

Competing Priorities: From Naïve to Wise

In coming-of-age stories, protagonists lose their innocence by realizing that bad things can happen and circumstances will not always favor them. In the story of the ExCEL Model, this happened when we faced one of the threats to sustainability: competing priorities.

Competing priorities interfere with timelines that aim to complete project deliverables on time and on budget. Competing priorities affect effectiveness.

Everybody has competing priorities. Due to the very nature of our target population, the schools we work with have many competing priorities. Nothing proved more of a competing priority than the COVID-19 pandemic. Schools closed. The university issued a mandate to cease research operations that required travel or working in schools. We went into triage.

We considered how to handle the situation both diplomatically and with empathy. First, we neutralized the urgency. We communicated with our district sponsors to inform them of the university mandate to cease activities. Not only was it a requirement but we also did not want our project to be an additional stressor on top of highly uncertain and emotionally charged circumstances. We kept tabs on what was happening where they were. On a very intermittent timeline and depending on the particular stressful or distressing news coming out of their area, we would reach out with a brief message wishing them well.

We analyzed our performance objectives for what we could continue to work on, given the existing conditions. Problem-based learning curriculum unit writing objectives rose to the top. Dissemination and publication writing surfaced as well. We laid groundwork to prepare to hit the ground running with implementation. We identified the two strategic deliverables that would make the most difference to accelerating implementation when schools opened up again. Both were related to professional learning and both became our priorities: completing the writing of the professional learning program as a comprehensive problem-based learning unit and creating a teacher guide for using the Cognitive Apprentice Rubric as a self-directed tool for teacher reflection.

We assessed our protocols and procedures. We updated and revised our protocols while also creating a few new ones. We organized our files. We created templates for data collection and communication.

Basically, we cleaned the closets and polished the railings. We did the deep cleaning that was difficult to get done when implementation was active.

Even after schools reopened and the university mandate was lifted, our work was vulnerable. Teachers were overwhelmed and substitute teachers were nearly impossible to find. Navigating this leg of the journey took patience, empathy, and prioritization. The payoff for the protagonist in losing innocence is gaining wisdom. Coping with COVID-19 complications taught us that sustainability is about fortitude. It taught us to acknowledge competing priorities and work within existing structures.

It is reasonable people are reluctant to take something like the ExCEL Model on in light of competing priorities. We hear "no" a lot. No is a form of feedback, not failure. No is a push to shift from problem-solving to problem-finding. It is not the end of the conversation, but rather it is the beginning of a negotiation. The negotiation being what is it going to take to turn that no into a maybe and that maybe into a yes? How can we make progress today? We tell ourselves, the best way we can be successful tomorrow is to be successful today.

Turnover: From Idealist to Realist

In coming-of-age stories, protagonists lose their idealism by realizing that life will not always be perfect. In the story of the ExCEL Model, this happened when we encountered another of the threats to sustainability: turnover. Turnover, both internally and with our participating districts, happened early on. Turnover affects fidelity.

Schools with the target population for our project experience high levels of turnover. It is an understandable concern, but it is often misunderstood. When turnover occurred at the teacher level, it would rattle principals. When turnover happened at the principal level, it would rattle our district sponsor. When turnover happened at the district sponsor level, it would rattle district leadership. When turnover happened on all of those levels at once, it would rattle us. That was when we shifted into high gear.

Principals were concerned about capacity. Frequently, their new hires were early-career teachers. Their worry was that the learning curve would be too steep. The assumption being that the number of years of teaching or experience with teaching PBL equated to success with PBL implementation. A variation of this concern about capacity played out with each role. District sponsors were worried about principal capacity, district leadership was worried about our district sponsor capacity, and so on. Inexperience raised doubts about capacity and bandwidth. When the number of teachers participating in the project who were also new hires reached a critical mass, principals wanted an exit ramp. This was reasonable, yet misguided. Interviews with strong PBL teachers revealed that they differed not by age, but in terms of their increased tolerance for ambiguity, change, and risk. Their increased capacity for reflective practice was also a factor in their success.

One component of the project was to examine the sustainability of the model in light of turnover. We came to anticipate when schools and districts might be considering withdrawing. We began to recognize the signs and symptoms. Our team employed strategic steps to recapture commitment and sustain participation.

We reconnected our district participants to the alignment of our project and the district strategic plan. We revisited the mission and goals of the project to tap into their vision and identity as educators. We targeted the scale of the project to make it more manageable. We developed a customized support plan to address the most critical and urgent stressors. We assured our districts that we would show up and our team would be there every step of the way. We would not disappear. We would address every question, concern, and comment. And then we did.

In an ideal world, every teacher, principal, district supervisor, and superintendent would see the ExCEL Model as the core of their work. They would set aside all other interests to give it their undivided attention. In reality, there is no priority in education that will ever serve as a singular focus. Navigating this part of the journey required an acceptance of our and others' limitations and strengths.

The payoff for the protagonist in losing idealism is gaining resilience. Coping with turnover taught us that sustainability is about tolerating ambiguity until a plan is formed. It grounded us in a growth perspective with continuous improvement as the engine. It moved us from considering success to be a product of achievement to success also being a product of service. It taught us to build an invested team and create infrastructure that superseded institutional knowledge at the individual level. It pushed us to find the champion. People often argue whether change takes place top down or bottom up. And whether change is most effective working from the outside or inside. Both are false dichotomies. Change happens in all directions at once. It is layered. We work on many levels. Anyone, at any point, can be the champion and elevate the mission.

Scale: From Immature to Mature

In coming-of-age stories, protagonists lose their immaturity by experiencing cognitive dissonance and learning to respond and react intentionally. In the story of the ExCEL Model, this happened when we faced the final major threat to sustainability: scale. Scale affects efficiency.

When schools reopened during the COVID-19 emergency, substitutes were, for all intents and purposes, nonexistent. Yet, we had a prerequisite two-day professional learning for teachers that we had spent the entire pandemic preparing. Assuming the substitute shortage was temporary, our district sponsors shouldered heroic efforts recruiting central office personnel to fill classrooms that teachers had left vacant to attend our professional learning. The substitute situation eased up eventually. But what became clear to our district partners before it became clear to us was that the pandemic was a one-way ticket. We were not returning to a time when schools could spare the time, energy, and resources to allow teachers to attend a full two-day professional learning session. We needed a transition plan. To do that, we needed to listen to our district partners' truths.

If, ultimately, our goal was for the ExCEL Model to work in the real-world context of actual schools across varied environments, then it needed to be nimble. Everything nonessential needed to be whittled away. The transition plan was a valuable half step. It gave us an opportunity to implement what we had developed a few more times in order to collect information that could help us understand what we could compact. Variability in our districts helped carve out agility. It pointed to what carried over across different environments. Using this information to guide us, revisions were made.

We produced the professional learning program in three formats: a one-day in-person version, a hybrid version, and an all-online version. Not only was this a more efficient evolution of the professional learning program because of the addition of these new formats but it was also more flexible. This was because we listened and accepted our district partners' truths about the real-world conditions and constraints they were facing. Navigating this part of the journey took the ability to hold two opposing ideas in mind at the same time and understand that both were true in relativity. Navigating this leg of the journey took curiosity and open-mindedness.

The payoff for the protagonist in losing immaturity is gaining acumen. Competing priorities and turnover bring the scale of the project into sharp focus. Coping with how the scale of the project affects efficiency pushed us to address all-or-nothing thinking, develop intellectual humility, and let go of perfectionism.

Testing, Scaling, and Sustaining

When we look back to make sense of what we have done, we see developmental phases. First, there was the testing phase. We identified the critical elements of the model and tested them. The systemic model emerged from this phase. Next, there was the scale-up phase. We examined how the model held up across contexts. That launched the sustainability phase, during which we measured the durability of the model to inform our understanding of the longevity of the model.

Each phase was characterized by an increasing laser-like focus on process. Responding with an understanding of multiple perspectives, a growth mindset, and quantitative and qualitative data made the model increasingly more efficient, effective, and accessible. Supporting teachers to do their job well so that they could support students to do their job well added value and meaning. Understanding what was meaningful added layers to the model's sustainability.

Change will continue to happen. The model needs to be flexible enough to keep up. That means turning it over to schools. Giving schools ownership, accountability, and authority over implementing and adapting the model for their individual contexts. Evolution is how the model will be sustained.

Building a Pipeline

Applying the ExCEL Model is like putting a steel beam into a house. It is putting access to challenging curriculum and instruction at the heart of schools within core subject curriculum during the regular course of the school day. It is a big lift. We do not expect it to happen overnight. It has never existed in isolation. It has always been a product of those who have come before us and it will continue to be dependent on those who come after us. It has always relied on the cooperation of schools.

What we do with the model will fold into the fabric of all that is known. Accepting our part, understanding where we begin and where we end, and knowing when to let go are important parts of our contribution. If we had not reached this understanding, we would not have evolved. The pipeline of succession would not persist.

We hope that reading this book has inspired you to be a part of the pipeline. Whether your experience of this book was that of a professional self-help book, manual, research brief, or journal article, we hope that we have helped you to try something new or different, support the professional growth of your team and school, identify changes that will make your gifted program equitable, or ground your work in evidence. Mostly, we hope that we have helped to make your life and your students' lives better. Rainer Maria Rilke (2021) said, "Live the questions now. Perhaps you will then gradually, without noticing it, live along some distant day into the answer." Creating equity is about the questions you ask, the process of discovery, and the meaning you make from it. This is how we came of age with the ExCEL Model.

References

Brown, A. L. (1992). Design experiments: Theoretical and methodological challenges in creating complex interventions in classroom settings. *The Journal of the Learning Sciences, 2*(2), 141–178. https://doi.org/10.1207/s15327809jls0202_2

Horak, A., & Shaklee, B. (2019). *Project E-Ignite*. U.S. Department of Education, Javits Gifted and Talented Students Education Grant Program.

National Association for Gifted Children. (2019). *2019 Pre-K–Grade 12 gifted programming standards*. http://www.nagc.org/sites/default/files/standards/intro%202019%20Programming%20Standards.pdf

Rilke, R. M. (2021). *Letters to a young poet*. Courier Dover Publications.

Shaklee, B., & Horak, A. (2014). *Project ExCEL*. U.S. Department of Education, Institute of Educational Sciences, Javits Gifted and Talented Students Education Grant Program.